Pelican Books
Children in their Primary S

Henry Pluckrose was educated at Henry Thornt...
Clapham, and at the College of St Mark and St Jo...
Chelsea. Since 1968 he has been headteacher at the Prio... ...ow.
Weston Primary School, London. He has lectured on
aspects of English primary education not only in Britain,
but in North America, Europe and Singapore and Hong
Kong as well. His principal concerns have been in the
fields of art and environmental education and he has
written over fifty books for children and numerous books
for parents and teachers on these topics. He has written,
with Peter Wilby, *The Condition of English Schooling*,
also published in Penguins. In 1976 he was made a Fellow
of the College of Preceptors, and is currently serving on
the Council for National Academic Awards. From 1968
to 1978 he was editor of the monthly magazine *Art &
Craft in Education*.

Henry Pluckrose is married and has three children, all of
whom have attended state primary and comprehensive
schools.

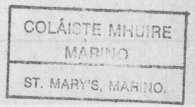

Children in their Primary Schools

Henry Pluckrose

Penguin Books

Penguin Books Ltd, Harmondsworth,
Middlesex, England
Penguin Books, 625 Madison Avenue,
New York, New York 10022, U.S.A.
Penguin Books Australia Ltd, Ringwood,
Victoria, Australia
Penguin Books Canada Ltd, 2801 John Street,
Markham, Ontario, Canada L3R 1B4
Penguin Books (N.Z.) Ltd, 182–190 Wairau Road,
Auckland 10, New Zealand

First published 1979
Copyright © Henry Pluckrose, 1979
All rights reserved

Made and printed in Great Britain by
Hazell Watson & Viney Ltd,
Aylesbury, Bucks
Set in Linotype Times

In Memoriam

Frank Peacock, Teacher and Friend

1909–1977

'I suppose it will be absolutely necessary to educate our masters . . . From the moment you entrust the masses with power their education becomes an imperative necessity. You have placed the government of this country in the hands of the masses and you must therefore give them an education'.

Robert Lowe on the Second Reform Bill, 1867

'At the heart of the educational process lies the child. No advances in policy, no acquisitions of new equipment have their desired effect unless they are in harmony with the child, unless they are fundamentally acceptable to him'.

The Plowden Report, 1967

Contents

Acknowledgements

I would like to record my thanks to the people who have helped me in the presentation of this book: Jill Norman of Penguin Books for her helpful advice on the preparation and revision of the manuscript; Frank Coles, sometime Senior Tutor of the College of St Mark and St John, for his perceptive comments and suggestions; and Cicely Tipple for her careful preparation of the typescript.

Preface

'Education is the whole realm of human consciousness, action and possibility.'   *James Agee*

In 1977 the Prime Minister, James Callaghan, launched a great debate on education. His speech may have been determined by political opportunism, but it was also timely. Although it focussed attention upon the quality of schooling enjoyed by our children, it also served to highlight a more fundamental issue. Is the principal purpose of education to provide our factories, workshops and offices with a reasonably competent work force or should our schools have a more distant, less tangible aim? If mastery of facts and the manipulation and application of 'rules' (for example in number or written English) is regarded as the yardstick of the educated child, we are in danger of debasing the meaning of the word 'education'. If, on the other hand, our schools are producing young people who are illiterate and innumerate (but who are considered 'creative' by their teachers) then this too suggests a naivety quite out of keeping with the reality of life in the twentieth century.

Thankfully neither of these viewpoints is representative of the thinking which underlies the majority of our schools. Essentially the great debate has been about the emphasis which should be placed on these two aspects of the education process. Should we concentrate upon facts and techniques (but not the sure knowledge) that the young adult, so programmed, can develop his own interests or should we devote a considerable proportion of school resources into developing the 'whole child'? Some educationalists go further than the latter and suggest that schools should also help children to cope with the unemployment (or under-employment) which is likely to be characteristic of our society for the forseeable future.

While the merits of these two viewpoints may have nothing to do with five, seven or eleven year olds, our primary and middle schools can not but be influenced by the general climate of public opinion. If some schools are thought to be failing industry, if children are not meeting the academic demands made upon them, then the backlash falls upon all, almost without exception. That schools are no more than a reflection of our society and that children are moulded by a whole variety of contemporary attitudes shaped in home and street as well as in school is conveniently forgotten.

This can be illustrated in a number of ways. Children, we are told, are not reading any more. However, the average print run of a first novel or the number of bookshops in the United Kingdom suggest that adults are not reading very much either. Both these statements are built upon half truths. Probably children are not reading as much fiction as they were twenty years ago, but they are buying and using more information books than they ever have before. Then I note that the standards of morality in our schools have fallen, that the Christian ethic is no longer respected or taught and that drink, drugs and sex (hallmarks of our acquisitive and permissive society) are undermining the young. If this is true (which I would dispute) why are there not similar criticisms of advertising campaigns for promoting the glamour of alcohol and tobacco, television for bringing the excitement of violence into our homes, newsagents for displaying soft porn for all to see, or publishers for making money by marketing it? Or again should I, as headteacher, be expected to punish a child for swearing when his mother, complaining about her son's language, observes to us both, 'If he bleeding well swears again, I'll beat the little bugger senseless.'

These examples should not be taken as a criticism of parents, nor should they be regarded as providing an excuse for sloppy teaching or wayward learning. However, they should be regarded as a criticism of the double standards which pervade our society. It is as though we want our schools to provide something *we think* we had at school; time may have wrought a change in the social, political and economic climate, but schools and education should be changeless.

Schools, in a Western democracy, occupy an impossible position: they exist in the present and yet they are invariably compared with the past. We, the adults, have all been to school, enjoyed success or suffered failure; our memories of schooling remain with us to colour our responses to the education our children are receiving, to give us a personal yardstick with which to beat the more outrageous fancies of the contemporary academic world. We want our children to be like us, to respect our values, to move easily in our culture, to respond to our view of life. We have a desire to do well by them, to give them the best possible start in life. But we tend to forget that our children are not growing up in the world of our own childhood, that for better or worse things have changed, that our time is not their time. In order for them to grow and develop fully we need to allow them to live in the time of their own childhood which we can share with them but never enter.

This problem – of understanding the nature of children – has always been with us. John Wesley (1703–91), quoting his mother, thought that children needed to have their spirit broken at the earliest possible stage in their development. 'Break their will betimes. Begin this great work before they can run alone, before they can speak plain, before they can run at all. Break their will if you would not damn the child.'

Contrast this with an equally extreme viewpoint from the headteacher of Summerhill School, A. S. Neill: 'My view is that a child is innately wise and realistic. If left to himself without adult suggestion of any kind he will develop as far as he is capable of developing.'

Control or freedom, firm discipline or paternalistic indulgence, these elements continue to puzzle – and trouble – all who have responsibility for children. The English primary school clearly illustrates these tensions. Should we control the teaching methods and curricula of our schools or should we allow teachers even greater freedom than they have enjoyed hitherto? What do children do in school all day – play or work? And what is the difference? What is creative English and how can it be different from any other form of written English that the children attempt? Why do primary schools encourage freedom of expression in poetry, paint, dance and movement when the reality of the adult world is quite the reverse? How have English primary schools achieved an international reputation for child-centred learning and is this reputation justified? To answer the questions adequately we need to examine the schools in some detail, their approaches to timetabling and curriculum planning, the expectations of the teachers, the needs of the children who attend them.

In preparing the text I have become more and more aware how impossible is my task. I cannot define an English primary school, for each school is different, following a syllabus its staff have prepared to a timetable of their own making. Nor can I list any but the most general aims – though I can point to specific achievements. Compare this to a recent visit I made to Alberta, where I was presented with a booklet which set out 'goals' or twenty-eight basic aims of elementary education for the children of the province.

I hope I have managed to provide a framework which will help all who live alongside young children to understand them better, to understand how teachers are trying to meet their needs, and how we should be as critical of schools which don't allow children to live fully as we are of schools that debase literacy, numeracy or the social graces. But if my book is directed towards parents, I also hope it will prove useful to students of social science and to visitors to England who wish to discover more about our schools and colleges.

Perhaps at a time when talk of devolution fills the air I should end on a parochial note. I have deliberately used the word 'English' to describe the primary schools I write about. In Scotland the scene is quite a different one, and my knowledge of schools in Wales is insufficient for me to incorporate them in a book such as this.

One other deliberate omission I must record – before my critics do so! I have not included a detailed analysis of the nursery or play school movements. This is not to deny their significance or the part that they have played in the education of the young child, but rather that space prevents me from giving them the detailed comment they deserve. Finally I must state, as a teacher employed by the Inner London Education Authority, that the Authority is in no way responsible for the opinions expressed above – or in the pages which follow.

December 1977   *Henry Pluckrose*

Part One *Children, Schools and Schooling*

1 Looking at Children

Recently I took a group of ten and eleven year olds to the Tudor and Stuart rooms at the National Portrait Gallery. One boy, amazed at the clothes which the children of the rich were expected to wear, observed, 'Did they expect children to be children in those days, or simply be small-sized grown-ups?' Tony (who made the remark) was a tough, independent child who found it hard to picture a world which lacked the contemporary comforts provided by tee shirt, jeans and training shoes, the Saturday tensions which came from supporting a struggling football team and the daily excitements of skate-boarding.

The phrase 'small-sized grown-ups' has lodged itself in my memory, if only because our expectations of childhood are so different from those of our ancestors. Today we allow our children in the belief that by so doing they are more likely to mature into adults whose confidence in themselves has not been eroded.

To talk of childhood in these terms, however, implies that it is possible to define the peculiar qualities that make children different from adults. Indeed it could even be argued that by advancing such a premise we are in danger of attributing to childhood a 'magic', a specialness that might appeal to dreamers but have little relevance to the harsh realities of our modern world.

Let us look for a moment at the young child entering school. Are there qualities which we could isolate, which appear to be present in the majority of five year olds, girls as well as boys? The quality I noticed when faced with a class of four and five year olds for the first time was their physical energy. I found myself in charge of this group almost by accident. Their teacher was away, and I was drafted into her place. I had, at this time, taught for ten years, and, although my experience had until this moment been with older children, it was felt that I should be able to cope. The realization of my personal inadequacy came as something of a shock. These five year olds were nothing like the responsible and responsive ten year olds with whom I usually worked. They did not want to be confined to space, to predetermined activities, to be bound by my suggestions. They were polite enough, they respected my position as teacher but, in a kindly way, were quite dismissive. 'Obviously, you don't understand us and our way of doing things,' they seemed to be saying.

Somewhat chastened by the experience, I began to compare my approach to children with that of my colleagues who worked with young children. A number of differences were quickly apparent. The successful teachers based their work on the assumption that young children need firstly the security which comes from a loving relationship, and that this relationship is built upon trust and respect. When such a climate had been established, great care was taken in the fabric of the classroom. There was order; things had a place. Underpinning this physical order was an organizational one: 'we always do this,' and the 'we always' applied to the way children moved from the classroom to the hall or to the time of day that the rabbit had its bedding changed.

Lest it appear to my readers that these two elements, security and order, typified a particular style of formal teaching, I must disabuse them. These elements were observable in every class where children were learning and were happy. Some of the teachers were working in a traditional way, others were following a much more informal programme. But in each situation the children were respected and they knew and understood the way of life within their classroom.

I then began to look for other common elements. I had failed because I had been ill-prepared for the pure physical energy of young children. They need to express themselves in words and in action, to move as they work. Nowadays classrooms are usually arranged deliberately to enable movement between water tray and book corner, painting table and Wendy house.

This indicates another aspect of the young child. He is an individualist. John may be building with bricks, and Mary dressing up, but I 'want to do writing and that's what I'm going to do'. The organization of many an infant classroom may look, to the casual observer, so loose as to be almost non-existent. But in its very looseness lies its strength, because it enables John, Mary and Peter to follow their particular interests at the time and pace appropriate to them.

Young children, of course, are not as bound by time as are the adults in their lives. In the pre-school years the passing of time was marked by what happened: getting up, mid-morning sleep, going shopping, watching children's television, bath time and bed time. How long children spent on an activity depended more upon their interest in it than upon the ticking of a clock. The self-evident truth of this has not been lost on perceptive teachers, who try to provide, through their timetabling, opportunity for children to immerse themselves in an activity, to *use* time (rather than make them become the slave of it).

If children are working on different levels and on different activities within the same classroom space, it will have to provide a wide range of materials, both structural (like bricks) and tactile (like paint and clay), for the children to use. Some of these materials may relate to reading, some to mathematics, some will aim to fire the imagination, others to develop powers of reasoning. But there will also be objects (perhaps carefully displayed) whose sole purpose is to awaken interest, delight the eye, encourage discussion. For above all, the young child is curious; the world, for a five year old is a very new place. This excitement with the real world (and even in a drab slum street the world is often vibrant with life) is reflected through the young child's use of his senses. He touches, smells, tastes, listens, sees. He wants to explore with all his senses. Looking, or hearing an adult describe an object, a place, or an event, is not enough. Personal involvement seems to be the way he learns. 'We went to the zoo. I held a snake. It was smooth and dry and had a sharp tongue and a bright eye.' John, aged six, ended his writing by observing 'Snakes don't smell.'

Curiosity leads to questioning. The why, hows and wheres of

pre-school days continue, the questions becoming more and more acute. By encouraging children to talk and to express their thoughts and feelings, the successful infant teacher is using language to extend the children's understanding of the world, making it, in the words of T. S. Eliot, 'the fluid in which all else is suspended'.

But a child does not enter school only to talk, to make and do, to have his curiosity aroused and satisfied, to be given space to move. He also goes to learn. No doubt he has had school presented to him as a place where he will quickly learn to do sums, unravel the meaning of words and sentences. He will therefore have certain expectations of his teachers and of his school. *He will want to learn.* This characteristic, I feel, has been temporarily lost beneath a welter of new words and phrases. 'Motivation' (a well-loved word in many an education lecturer's phrase book) has been used to describe almost everything except the innate desire of the young to master the key activities of the society into which they are born. Children want to learn to read and write, to use books, to do 'real' work. They need to feel that the school day has a plan and a purpose (and so do their parents). When modern methods fail to convince parents of their relevance to the educational process, it is often a reflection on the inability of the teachers to show that work and play are not necessarily different (and conflicting) activities. A parent disenchanted with her child's school will, like as not, produce a disenchanted child and a disenchanted child will not learn as successfully as an enthusiastic one.

In the seven years between five and eleven subtle changes occur. Eleven year old Mark will continue to be as interested in the happenings of home and school as his five year old sister. But he will also be developing specific interests which might well seem to be all-consuming. One eleven year old I knew showed little interest in any school subject except electricity and circuits, and another rather jaded boy came to life when he was introduced to pottery and a wheel, a girl for whom home and school were equally frustrating places quite changed her attitude and outlook when she discovered that she had considerable ability in music and began to realize it. The intensity and depth of these pre-adolescent interests can be seen in many primary school classes today, particularly where children are encouraged to follow their individual interests by studying in depth such things as ornithology, chess, music, literature, history or mathematics.

The ten year old, so enthused, is also capable of considerable intellectual effort, and this is not only reflected in the quality of his work, but also in the length of time which he is prepared to devote to the activity. Again, if children are not restricted by a narrow timetable, they will not feel bound by time. Mandy I remember as a child who would quite happily work for three days, uninterrupted, on a mathematical project, Jacqueline as a girl who knew more about the intricacies of spinning and weaving than many an adult. Should I worry (as a parent or teacher) at such an excessive amount of time spent upon such singular activities? Or, should I be comforted by the fact that to do anything worth while (whether writing a book, researching the statistics for a graph to show population in Islington between 1801 and 1977 or preparing the warp for a twenty-four-inch double-headed loom) takes time, effort and a degree of quixotic devotion to the task in hand? This sharpening of interests also reflects itself in the passion which many children have in collecting things – from stamps and first-day covers to Victorian bric-a-brac and train numbers.

The eleven year old will also have begun to realize the nature of sexuality. The small child is, in the main, asexual. That is not to say that male and female role play will not suggest that boys and girls have an awareness of their sexual differences. Such role play is, in my opinion, superficial. Boys (unless they are actively discouraged by the adults in their lives) enjoy playing with dolls, dressing up and doing household chores such as dusting and cooking. Girls, given the opportunity, will play with trains, make forts for imaginative battles and enjoy the rough and tumble of horseplay.

The distinction between the sexes in our society is now more confused than ever it has been. In school I notice that girls seem a little more combative than they once were, more willing to attempt activities which were once the preserve of the boys. This blurring is continuing into adolescence and many secondary schools are including 'home economics' as a compulsory subject for boys, while girls are being introduced to such things as metalwork, woodwork and technical drawing.

It is in the intellectual sphere that the biggest changes are to be observed. The eleven year old has reached the stage in his development where fact and fantasy are clearly separated, where imagination can be disciplined, where such things as time past can be related to time present, where 'knowing' has taken the place of intuition. This latter observation is nowhere more clearly demonstrated than in the field of mathematics. A five year old will continually count out her beads to answer a sum. '8 + 2 makes 10 this time,' her actions seem to say, 'but will 2 + 8 make 10 as well?' The consistency of laws of nature is continually questioned by the young child. For the emerging adolescent, such laws, once understood, are accepted and applied. By the time the child leaves primary school he will begin to be capable of abstract thought.

Intellectual development is probably the one area which the adults in their lives find the most difficult to handle. We are flattered by our children's sophistication but resent the challenge it can bring. Children resent unfairness at five. But because they are small they can do little to counter our lack of justice. By eleven many children are prepared to challenge our adult view of things, to question our values, to comment on our inconsistencies. Their growing verbalization, their ability to argue and to present their viewpoint (however extravagantly expressed), suggest that we need to handle this stage of their development with particular care. In the school in which I work, for example, we have instituted a school council, a small body elected by the children themselves to represent their viewpoint. The discussions have been many and varied, from the care of the grounds, the possible development of a small zoo and expenditure on a wild garden, to the possibility of girls playing football and the choice of paperbacks in the school library. For this council to work successfully the adults involved must respect the children's decisions and to give them support when extricating themselves from unwise ones. Growing up means taking decisions; it also means coping with mistakes.

Intellectual development goes hand in hand with social development. The child of five or six is essentially a loner, working and playing in company with other children, but not really co-operating to any extent with his fellows. He is often possessive of his own equipment and materials, unwilling to share. This possessiveness tends to diminish and by nine or ten most children are quite happy to share; communal use of personal as well as community equipment is an accepted part of school life.

During the primary years, another significant point to be considered is that children are creatures of the moment. They work best, and most successfully, when the objectives are clear, comprehensible, immediate. To offer Penny a cycle 'if she does well in her exam' is not likely to make her perform any better – especially if the examination is some time ahead; the gaining of gold stars towards a house cup (a long-term aim) is not likely to make Jim any more mindful to devote himself to work – the star on his work for today's achievement will give him much greater satisfaction.

Bound up with this need to live and work for the immediate moment is enthusiasm. At no other time in life does the human being display such enthusiasm for learning, for living, for finding out. Many parents will testify how a request from a popular and trusted teacher will cause a child to get to school half an hour early to clear out the rabbit run, or to forgo playtime and hometime to tidy a cupboard or repair some books. Such enthusiasm does not only apply to manual work. A gifted teacher can persuade her class that Norman England is a fascinating topic to study, or that, next to the World Cup, magnetism is the most significant aspect of contemporary society. Young children absorb information with facility and enthusiasm and this removes from primary teaching some of the tensions which come with the adolescent years. Primary school teachers teach children, not subjects; it is of paramount importance, therefore, that we present to children things to learn which are of value. It would be so easy to project viewpoints which were unacceptable to the broad majority of our society – on the Irish problem, for example, on politics, on emotive issues like contraception or immigration. To its credit, the teaching profession in England, despite the considerable freedom it enjoys, has never been accused of abusing its trust.

All that I have written so far must be seen as indicating something of the nature of the primary school child. My observations relate to the typical child attending the typical school from the typical family. To write so ambiguously serves to underline the difficulty we have when describing a human being – be he five or fifty. There are some children whose concentration span at seven is better than that of most eleven year olds; there are others who at twelve still find it difficult to relate to their friends at anything but a rudimentary level. There are some children whose curiosity never seems to have awakened; there are others for whom book learning and the mastery of facts transcends all other aspects of their life in school. We cannot reduce human beings to a mean. No two children are alike; not even children from an identical background have an identical pattern of development. All that can be said is that children – as they develop – go through certain clearly identifiable stages and have, as they develop, certain clearly identifiable interests, methods of problem solving, patterns in the mastery of basic physical skills. In planning the way a five year old girl, for example, is to spend her day in school we need to know what sort of things to expect from her and what sort of experiences she needs of us. So, although each child is different and unique, each child as she grows and develops is also very like her neighbour. To school each child will bring something of her family and the experiences of her pre-school years; in school each child will develop skills and realize her innate potential.

Nowhere can the individual pattern of development be so clearly seen and a child's strengths and weaknesses identified as in his play. It has been said that play is the most significant activity of childhood. Play, however, is a much misunderstood word. To suggest that play is an integral part of schooling is, at first glance, something of a paradox. Schooling implies discipline and control, a steady imput of carefully ordered experiences. Play, on the other hand, suggests freedom and experiment, with little adult intervention.

This somewhat simplistic view ignores completely the nature of the growing child. From birth a baby explores his world. This exploration will be guided by the adults in his life, but his response to the experiences which come his way will be intuitive. He will learn by touching, smelling and tasting: he will learn by listening and looking.

Early play is largely a solitary occupation. The child's play is very much a struggle to come to terms with the world in which he lives – to make his bricks balance, to push his baby-walker without falling over, to hammer pegs into a wooden board, to make marks on paper. Studying a toddler at play should be an essential part in all teacher training courses. The student would soon come to realize that play has many of those qualities which are integral to any successful education process – commitment to the activity for its own sake, concentration and repetition being the most significant. Adults find it difficult to appreciate that play – for young children – is a continuous activity. It is not an activity, like washing or eating, which is defined by time, place or circumstance. It is for this reason that many parents – and teachers – despair because the expensive, well-designed toys they have thoughtfully and lovingly provided are so rarely played with – and that junk holds unbelievable magic for their offspring.

Play will teach children something of the nature of wood and sand, water and paper, plastic and fabric, but it will do far more: it will help extend concentration and develop manipulative skills. Tools (often created by the child to meet his particular need) will be introduced to enable the activity to be further extended.

Through play, children's language is developed and extended: in play they learn how to co-operate with others – and the social penalties that are incurred when they fail to do so. Imaginative play enables children to work out their fears and anxieties and helps them to come to terms with the world in which they live. Jean, aged seven, was not odd because she spent every moment of her spare time playing hospitals and curing sick dolls. It would have been much odder had she not used this means to reassure herself. Her mother had been in and out of hospital for several years. She had always survived the operations. In playing out her anxiety Jean expressed it, and came some way to facing the realization that one day her mother might not emerge.

In the early years of schooling the significance of play is now widely recognized (even when I went to school we were allowed to take toys on Friday afternoons!). Too often, however, the middle years of schooling are so structured, that play * – deep involvement in an activity for its own sake – is virtually ignored.

Somewhat surprisingly, those schools which might be considered the most formal elevate certain elements of play. The ritual of team games emphasizes the character-forming aspects of play – keeping to the rules, co-operating with team mates, accepting disciplines, losing with grace, winning without conceit. Great emphasis is placed upon the enjoyment which comes from playing well; playing well will involve the mastery of specific skills through repetition and practice.

I wonder, however, why these particular sentiments are not seen as having even greater relevance to other areas of a child's life. Learning to read, for example, can be presented as an enjoyable activity which requires effort, concentration and practice: mathematics need not be drab and lifeless, for a child playing with Unifix mathematical blocks is both playing and learning.

In many areas of the primary school curricula, 'play' and 'work' are interchangeable terms. To present 'work' in an informal way is not to make it 'play' (and thereby unacceptable). To present work as enjoyable is not immoral, nor is it reasonable to argue that, because many adults regard their work as tedious, children should be made to have similar feelings about

* Play was defined by Caldwell Cook in *The Playway* (published in 1917) as 'anything you did with your whole heart in it'.

theirs. But perhaps the most important thing which 'respect for play' has brought into the contemporary primary school is the acceptance that fear provides no motive for learning or working. We function best (and, therefore, are most likely to be able to take advantage of the opportunities for learning provided) when we are really interested and deeply involved.

Play – as outlined here – is not confined to childhood. It remains with us throughout our adult life. For some there will be commitment to traditional games such as cricket, bowls, football, chess or bridge. The 'play' element for others may be in photography, cooking, gardening, dressmaking, knitting, car maintenance, carpentry or home decoration. Grown men 'play' with the model trains that they have spent hours in building, grown women 'play' when they collect dolls or breed dogs. In watching children and adults play, it is interesting to note that much is learned from the activity itself, that play involves a degree of self-teaching.

A study of young children at play, whether in park or classroom, will also help us understand something of the nature of childhood, and this understanding will surely help us to cope with them better as parents and as teachers. We shall be made aware of the importance of words, for all children's pastimes even if they are alone, are liberally sprinkled with speech. Language (which is dealt with at some length in Chapter 5) is accompanied by *doing*. The primary school child is an activist – he loves to make, do and fashion. For this he needs the opportunity to use materials and the space in which to do so, and classrooms – and schools – reflect this. Paints, constructional toys, clothes for dressing up, card, paper, junk, jigsaws, bricks, sand, water, weaving looms and screen printing frames are now as common as were the slate and primer of my parents' school days.

Involvement with the sophisticated products of our technological society can lead to great bursts of learning. Moreover the realization that quite small children are able to use sophisticated equipment has resulted in something of a revolution in the classroom. Tape recorders, cameras, video machines and projectors are now found in most schools. What is particularly significant, however, is not that they are available as teaching aids, but that they are often used by the children.

The movement towards child-centred learning programmes in our schools has not escaped criticism. Some academics and politicians argue that to organize a school around the nature of children is simplistic and romantic. More important, such a programme is likely to ignore the central role of the teacher, that of turning egocentric infants into young people capable of benefiting from the intellectual rigours of secondary education. If, the argument continues, teachers spend their time watching and waiting for John or Mary to reveal interests which can be tapped and enriched they may well wait for ever. Teachers should be initiators rather than watchers. If this is a reasonable standpoint to adopt what was so wrong with traditional methods which relied more upon the teacher to determine moment-to-moment life within the classroom? 'A child,' one young student of education said to me, 'will never discover for himself that the world is round. Tell him and he'll know.'

Such observations neatly evade the central issue. Much of the success enjoyed by the gifted teacher stems from her ability to fire interests which already exist. As a child I loved the patterns in sound which words made when manipulated by a gifted story-teller or a sensitive poet. How much easier it was for me to learn when, at the age of fifteen, I was taught by a teacher of English who recognized my interest and fed it. How much more efficiently I learned, how much more exciting and rewarding became his task of teaching. A personalized example such as this might seem to be an insignificant contribution to the discussion were it not for the fact that it can be echoed by the majority of my readers. We learn best when our interests are identified, extended and enriched by someone who has greater experience than we do ourselves. The teachers we fondly remember from our school days are the ones who did precisely this.

Child development is not a new study, but it is only in the last thirty years that its researches have had much impact upon schools. As a result teachers of young children have been encouraged to rely less on intuition and more upon observation. Children will still learn facts, be told that the world is round. What has changed is that such information is presented in a context which is appropriate to their age and understanding.

In recent years I have visited primary schools in eastern, southern and western Europe, the United States and the Far East. As one would expect, each country I visited has evolved its own style of education for the early years of childhood. In some countries (Yugoslavia, for example) the curriculum that the schools follow is predetermined. A committee of each republic decides upon content and method, and the responsibility of the headteacher is to see that this defined curriculum is taught in an approved and acceptable way. Thus each year-group in each school within the republic of Serbia, for example, will be following an identical syllabus. Central control on content and teaching style has, it is argued, certain advantages. It means that a child can be transferred from one school to another with little disruption to his learning programme, that teachers are discouraged from attempting experimental approaches, that every parent knows what programme his child is undergoing in school. Control of education to this degree also has certain dangers. Curriculum control can mean that texts are prepared from a particular political standpoint, to promote sectarianism or to further religious prejudice.

In Sweden the central government also offers guidelines to teachers, but they do not have to be slavishly followed. Experiments in teaching method are encouraged but, as a senior member of the Swedish education service remarked to me, 'Once we produce a document our teachers tend to regard it as definitive. Anyway it's easier to teach from a book. There *is* freedom of approach, but I'm afraid that many of our teachers feel free not to move from the guidelines.'

Both the Yugoslavs and the Swedes would probably argue that one of the aims of their system of government is to produce an egalitarian society, where all children are given an equal opportunity to develop their skills and gifts to the fullest possible extent. But each school system operates within restraints. In Yugoslavia they are clearly political and accepted as such. In Sweden they are less obvious, but it remains virtually impossible for a Swedish parent to choose the primary school his child will attend: the local school is your school whatever you feel about its quality or the relevance of its programme ... All of which has the effect of stifling experiment and school-based curriculum innovation.

In the United States the grade system operates. At six the child enters Grade 1, moving up a grade each year to Grade 12 before leaving Senior High School at eighteen. The protagonists for the grade system stress that it enables nationwide standards to be maintained, checking (by yearly exams) on pupils' progress (and, incidentally, the efficiency of schools and teachers) and ensuring a degree of equality of opportunity from state to state. Certainly the grade system produces some uniformity of curriculum content (the big publishers vie with each other to produce texts for the school market which will be as acceptable in the deep South and the mid-West as in California and New York). There are experiments to mix the grades, to break down the arbitrary barriers that the grade system has created, but experimental schools are the exception rather than the rule.

This is not to say – in any of the countries I have mentioned so far – that consensus agreement of curriculum content and teaching style has produced equality of opportunity. It seems to me that accident of birth still plays too great a part in a child's educational development – whether he is born in the capitalist West or the communist East. A child born of caring parents in New Yorks' South Bronx would have much less opportunity to make educational progress than were the same parents fortunate enough to be living in Greenwich, Connecticut, 160 km away. Similarly a factory worker in Belgrade would probably find better schools in Câcèk (a new industrial town some 240 km from Belgrade). Economic pressures upon local community resources seem to have as significant a part to play in a nation's educational provision as centrally determined policies, whatever the political persuasion of the government concerned.

In the third world, the prime object of education is to help the majority towards a degree of literacy and numeracy. The aim being more prescribed and simplistic, the methods used are, by Western standards, somewhat blunt. 'We have the task,' a member of the Hong Kong Education Service told me, 'of teaching an ever-expanding child population to read and write.' So when I visited school buildings which were used to house two schools (a morning school for 700 children and an afternoon school for another 700), I was not surprised to find that many of the subjects I take for granted were nowhere to be found on the timetable. Nor was I surprised to discover that in common with many third-world countries the training of teachers for primary school classes did not rank high on the list of priorities. Does the teacher need to have followed an advanced educational course to teach small children? Indeed, are complex organizational patterns appropriate to the needs of young children? These are questions that have been put to me in several developing countries and, in the terms of their particular stage of development, questions which are extremely difficult to answer.

There are few countries in the world where primary school teachers enjoy such freedom as they do in England. There are also few countries where the pattern of education is so complex. It is virtually impossible, as we have already seen, to define the primary school in terms of a centrally imposed structure. The local school might cater only for children of infant age, it might be a first school, or a junior mixed and infants school with a nursery attached, a middle school or simply a school catering for junior boys. There is no area in England that could be chosen to describe the school that best typifies our approach to the education of young children and it is this acceptance of variety that is perhaps as confusing to many parents as it is to overseas academics and educationalists.

But it would be dangerous to assume that the schools in England, despite their rich variety, are unaffected by economic pressures, shifts of political power or the expectations of the community they are there to serve. Some inner-city primary schools are following an integrated multi-culture programme (including Black studies) that would be inappropriate for children living in middle-class commuter-belt villages; some country schools follow rural science courses which would be inappropriate for their urban counterparts. Even where there is a volatile cosmopolitan population (as there often is in inner cities), schools cannot break away entirely from the restraints imposed by community expectations. The William Tyndale School in North London, whose problems filled the newspapers in the mid-seventies, was condemned because the staff (in the opinion of the *majority* of the parents) failed to meet their understanding of their children's needs. It was not condemned simply because it was experimental but rather because such experiments as were undertaken were seen to fail. Indeed it is difficult, on a casual visit to a school, to evaluate the unseen influence of the parents upon the curriculum and the general management of the school. It would be foolish, in my opinion, for a group of teachers to decide to implement curriculum change overnight. Change must be worked for with teachers and parents co-operating in the process. Confrontation in education occurs when one of the elements in the education process (teacher, parent, child) refuses to respond to the expectations or demands of one of the other elements. Parents – by and large – want similar things; the best possible all-round education for their children. Sadly teachers are not always able to explain how the methods they are adopting will accomplish this end.

Parents, of course, can influence the curriculum in a positive way too. A school which is fortunate to have adults working for it in a voluntary capacity is often able to provide valuable support in extending the range of activities the children can undertake. Clearing a piece of waste ground for a garden might not suggest curriculum innovation, but if for the first time inner-city children can begin to grow things, practice is being added to textbook learning. If the local authority bans school swimming and the PTA responds by building a swimming pool, then an area of the curriculum is preserved despite arbitrarily imposed financial restraint. If parents are prepared to support

teachers in all aspects of their work – and teachers show understanding and sympathy to parental expectations – much more
growth can occur within the school community.

All of this serves to illustrate political restraint at a parochial
level, but there are other levels of political involvement which
need to be borne in mind when looking at the organization of
any primary school. Firstly it is important to remember that
local political considerations (at county or metropolitan borough
level) will have some effect upon the education programme
undertaken by the schools. Political whimsy (for example, 'This
authority will have a tripart organization of first, middle and
high schools') will determine how each school is organized and
what are the expectations of the children and teachers within it.
If this should happen will the middle school teachers see themselves as professionals engaged in extending good primary
practice into the secondary age groups, or will their principal
aim be to relate secondary school aspirations and curricula to
children who, had they been in another authority, would have
been regarded and taught as third- and fourth-year *juniors*?

Similarly a local authority, through its elected council, could
demand yearly testing, selective screening, or programmes for
the gifted child; it could publish lists of successful schools;
introduce a voucher system. It could refuse to support areas of
the school curriculum (like swimming) and withdraw grants and
financial assistance for all manner of extra-curricular activities.

On the other hand, a neighbouring authority could behave in
quite the reverse fashion, encouraging innovation and new
teaching methods by building schools which support non-tradi-
tional teaching styles (such as open-plan schools), employing an
adequate advisory staff, providing houses for teachers and social
workers, and making funds available for community-based
developments.

Thus it is difficult to compare like with like. Individual institutions respond, amoeba-like, to local pressures, pressures
that are often hidden even from the most perceptive parent or
interested visitor.

Secondly, central government also exercises control. By

financial measures (such as devoting money to one aspect of education policy rather than to another) it can encourage or discourage development. If, for example, money is poured into the education programmes for decaying areas of inner cities rather than into the expansion of nursery education to cover all children aged between three and a half and five, a positive decision of discrimination is made. Such a decision could have far-reaching effects.

Or again central government might decide to raise the school leaving age to seventeen in an attempt to reduce youth unemployment or to raise the academic standards of young people entering industry. Unless such a change is given considerable financial support, the resources within schools will be strained. If in implementing such a programme teachers have to be redirected from one sector of education to another or the identical teaching force has to cope with a larger school population than it has done hitherto, the whole education programme (from 3 + to 18 +) will be affected.

On a less contentious level, government decisions of principle also produce subtle side effects within schools. Thus the abolition of selection at eleven freed the primary school of what many teachers felt to be a restrictive and inappropriate straitjacket, for it enabled schools to base their curriculum upon the needs of children rather than upon the demands of the examination, an examination which, by its very nature, was highly selective. The effect of this change was not unexpected. The needs of the majority of children were no longer submerged by the needs of the minority who would pass the examination. This resulted in a change of emphasis in the final years of a child's life in junior school; standards did not fall, but the measurement of what was happening in schools changed. It might be that in some cases insufficient thought was given to how best to meet the needs of the academically able (who up until this time had had rather more than their fair share of the educational expenditure), but on the whole the new freedoms which emerged as the result of the government decision to end selection have not been abused.

A third restraint upon the organization and teaching style of a school stems from what can only be described as 'tradition'. We expect our schools to do certain things – to teach children to read, write, use numbers, have some understanding of their culture. No headteacher, no class teacher, no lecturer in a college of education, no parent would dispute that these areas represent the 'core' around which the rest of the primary school curriculum should be built. Historically this has always been so. This means that there has been for many years a broad consensus on the aims, purpose and direction of primary education. Discussion is less about what we shall teach but how best to attain the goals society has set.

I make this point because it is too often assumed that the expectations of the educational right are wildly different from those of the educational left, that centralism in education is respectable because its advocates see it as embracing the best from both extremes. Such a view is an over-simplification. However a school is organized, however the teachers see themselves in political terms, the school will survive external pressures upon it in the long run only if the children who are leaving to enter secondary education are literate, numerate and socially aware.

Of course not all schools in one local authority area, not all schools across England, should be expected to achieve identical levels for their children. If the intake at five consists of children who have had a rich experience of language, we should expect them to perform better throughout their early years than children of families for whom English is a second language. Similarly if a school serves an area of slum housing where there is a high rate of unemployment, we should not expect the children to function at the same level as children of the same age who were fortunate to be born into economically secure families living in comfortable houses in pleasant streets. But although the long-term aspirations of the parents from these two extremes might be quite different (one being quite prepared for a daughter to leave school as early as possible for an unskilled job and marriage, while the other might regard anything less than university entrance as failure), the short-term aims (in my experience) are identical. The unshaven scrap merchant who came to inquire about his eight year old's progress in reading twenty years ago, when I was working in a school in London's dockland, asked the same questions of me as do the sophisticated, middle-class parents for whom I now work. The phrasing might be different, but the implication remains unchanged. 'How's Ethel doing then, with her reading and writing?' is not so very different from a request for 'an evaluation of Emily's language development,' or the observation that there's worry in the family 'because Timothy seems dyslectic'.

These are some of the factors that need to be borne in mind when considering the various organizational approaches to be found in contemporary primary schools. That there are wide differences in practice cannot be ignored; but these differences must always be seen within the context of the restraints within which our schools work. The 'freedom to be different' that teachers seem to enjoy is something of an illusion: whenever schools within the state sector have become too different they have invariably been closed or, by subtle re-allocation of staffing, their course has been gently altered towards conformity.

Thirty years ago the great debate in the education of young children centred upon the advisability of streaming. Streaming, of course, is something which all of us can understand. Most of today's parents went to streamed schools. The academically gifted children of a particular age group were taught in one class, the less academically endowed in another. The A-stream children were fed on an academic diet to enable them to cope with the examination at eleven, while the B-stream children progressed at a more measured, less exacting pace. Teachers and parents expected success from the A-stream, failure from the B-stream. Meanwhile both teachers and parents pretended to themselves that the children who were so graded didn't really know because, after all, they were only children.

All manner of educational reasons were found to justify the division. It was easier, for example, to teach children whose ability fell within certain defined bounds. Progress was quicker, for the bright were not held up by the slow, neither were the slow ignored because they were taught at a speed in a class that was right for them. The bright child, moreover, when challenged by other bright children would, through competition with his neighbours, be kept intellectually on edge. Little thought was given (because if streaming is accepted throughout a school exceptions are almost impossible to cope with) to those children who were at the bottom of the A-stream (and who might benefit from going slower) or those at the top of the B-stream (who might benefit from going faster). It was also difficult to accommodate children who were of above average ability in one area, such as maths, but who were below average in another, such as English. There was also a tendency to restrict the programme of the brighter children (making much of what they did examination-orientated) so that music, dance, drama and art played a less significant part in their curriculum. In some schools this reached almost farcical proportions. For example, I taught in one school where the children in each year were streamed into four classes, A, B, C and D. The class teachers for the A- and B-streams were the most senior and experienced members of staff, on the assumption that the best children deserved the best teachers. Each January, the day after the 11 + examinations, the fourth-year A teacher left his class and took over the third-year A-stream to begin what he described as 'grammar school preparation'. His fourth-year class were then expected to catch up on all the history, nature study, geography, music, art, craft and needlework they had missed in the previous three and a half years.

Reaction against streaming – when carried to these lengths – was to be expected. As more and more education authorities changed their transfer procedure (relying upon continuous assessment and verbal reasoning tests instead of 'once only' performances in English and mathematics under examination conditions) the weakness of streaming became apparent. If every child had interests and gifts, skills academic and mechanical, should he not be encouraged to develop these to the full in school?

Thus a classroom should provide an environment in which diversity could flourish. The aim of the primary school teacher was seen not as producing pupils who had undergone an identical number and language programme, but of allowing children to develop their own gifts while ensuring that language and numeracy developed at a pace appropriate to each individual within the class.

Such ideals are not always easy to put into practice. Undoubtedly the freeing of the curriculum after de-streaming illustrated how much more children could achieve in such things as art, science and music than we had previously expected of them, but there was a danger that the new freedoms might be abused. Children still needed to master mathematical skills, they still needed to be made aware of the rules of punctuation and spelling, they still needed support in the intermediate stages of reading.

Thus although streaming in junior schools is now comparatively uncommon, and the advantages of mixed-ability grouping are apparent for social as well as education reasons, teachers have never entirely rejected structuring learning by ability.

The idea of 'setting', taking children in groups to develop specific skills, was common in the all-age village school that our grandparents attended. Children, irrespective of age, were taught according to their ability. Since each child developed at a different pace, the 'set' to which he belonged could change over a school term or a school year. Rapid progress in mathematics, for example, might see one child move from a set of children working on basic number skills with whole numbers, to one working with decimals or vulgar fractions, while another child, less gifted, might remain with the same mathematical group for a term or even a year. The topic under consideration would obviously change over this period, but the presentation and content would closely relate to the teacher's awareness of the capacities of the children involved.

The mixed-ability class consists of a number of teacher-determined groups. These groups are used as the unit for teaching basic skills. The emergence of group teaching meant that the advantages of streaming (for formal teaching) were retained while allowing for maximum flexibility in the size and composition of the groups involved.

That 'setting' of mixed-ability groups requires more skill on the part of the teacher cannot be denied. Instead of working with one set of A/B-grade children, she might find that the abilities of her class ranged from A to E. Organization of such a diffuse range poses problems within the classroom; the need to appreciate the abilities of each child, his strengths and weaknesses, assumes paramount importance. No longer is the teacher protected by a set of clearly defined expectations, for each child will make different demands in each subject area, demands that are related to his ability, aptitude, experience and needs. The teacher of a mixed-ability class does not see herself simply as a disseminator of facts, but as a person who structures situations in which children learn.

It might well be the case, as critics of mixed-ability teaching have suggested, that this style imposes too great a strain upon the teacher of average ability, or the inexperienced teacher, and allows the lazy teacher too much scope for inefficiency. But to stifle progress on the grounds that the work force is not as competent as it might be is surely shortsighted. Our aim must be to make teachers and schools more effective. If this means that periods of regular retraining have to be built into each teacher's professional life (as recommended by the James Committee in 1972), there would be few objections from local education authorities, parents or professional bodies. In this connection it's worth noting that in terms of academic training today's young teachers have undertaken a more strenuous course than many of their older colleagues. Whereas graduates were rarely to be found on the staff of primary schools twenty years ago, nowadays they are quite commonplace. Indeed, three years' training (the exception ten years ago) is now the minimum requirement for certification. Therefore it is to be hoped – and expected – that the organizational problems which have emerged as a consequence of a more fluid style of schooling should not be regarded as insoluble. The new generation of young teachers (always provided the practice as well as the theory of education is a rigorous element of their training) should be more capable than their predecessors in implementing the best of contemporary practice.

Mixed-ability teaching is based upon the assumption that children learn at different rates, that each child has different interests, skills and abilities from his neighbour. Variety and diversity are characteristic of the classroom where mixed-ability teaching is practised. Some children may be working with number apparatus, others writing stories or collecting material for their own individual studies. If the class is in the infant age range, other children may also be playing with jigsaws, building with bricks, using sand and water to develop their understanding of such things as capacity and volume. In another corner of the room there may be children engaged in dramatic play in the Wendy house. While all this is going on there will probably be children reading and painting, or feeding the rabbit, the gerbils and the guinea pig.

There will be movement, there will be voices, and the teacher, although she may not be the visible focus of attention, will still be in control. While the majority of the class work independently of her, she is still the central hub around which the group revolve. Her role, of course, is not passive – for her interventions into the activities of the groupings that make up her class will be fundamental and far reaching, her effectiveness as a teacher and arbiter being enhanced in the process. The teacher's role, in the situation I have described, is a crucial one. She must clearly define the parameters within which her children work, she must ensure that individual and group activities are given appropriate time limits and that each child has a clear understanding of what is expected of him.

And yet this is not to suggest that the mixed-ability class will never come together to enjoy a corporate experience such as watching a television programme, or listening to a story or poem well read. Just as the pattern of individual and group activities undertaken will vary from day to day, so will the range of activities which are organized on a class basis. Sometimes class activities, such as a movement lesson, will be conceived by the teacher as the starting point for individual work; at other times the formal lesson provides the structure for clarifying, examining and relating tasks undertaken by individual children in the class.

The physical organization of a classroom where such a programme is undertaken has a character far different from the desk, blackboard and inkwell of our childhood memories. Because the learning programme is child-orientated (rather than teacher-dominated), the classroom is likely to be informally arranged, with tables, chairs and bookshelves designed for ease of movement and flexibility in use. Bookcases and mobile storage units that can act as room dividers, tables that fit together to seat groups of various sizes – the development of furniture that is purpose-built for childhood is one of the most significant developments in design in the educational post-war years. The furniture allows the materials which the children are using to be easily stored. Books, paint, paper, scissors, mathematical and scientific apparatus are accessible to children and staff. Just as a skilled craftsman organizes his studio so that the materials and tools he uses can be obtained as and when he needs them, so the skilled teacher organizes her room so that it becomes a workshop for children.

When visiting a school, therefore, it isn't necessary to see it full of children interacting with their teachers to arrive at some idea of the sort of programme that is being undertaken. Does the arrangement of rooms suggest mixed-ability teaching; is there evidence that certain areas of the room are kept for messy activities (like paint and clay) and that other parts of the room are specially equipped for mathematics or reading? What does the work on the walls tell us of the experiences that the class have had recently? How has the equipment been looked after? Are the reading books well used – even if they are old they don't have to look tatty! Has the room the feeling of a workshop in which children would be challenged?

The success of mixed-ability teaching, the realization that streamed classes were not necessarily the most effective way of educating young people, led to further experiment in school organization, experiment which to some extent had been practice born of necessity in many a small village school for generations.

If, it was suggested, streaming was of dubious value, was there any reason why children should be taught in tight year groups, where accident of conception and birth were the principal determining factors of school life? Thus if John were born on 30 August he would be regarded as a member of one year group, if he were born on 2 September another. There might be only three days difference in his age, but in his experience of the people he lived alongside these three days became the great divide.

Was there any reason, teachers asked, to regard the calendar year as having profound significance? If each child was regarded as unique, surely his uniqueness should be given the opportunity to flower in association with children of different ages. The realization that administrative convenience and tidyness is not a sound basis on which to organize a learning programme has not yet dawned on all teachers and all schools. But in many, family or vertical grouping has been introduced very successfully.

The term 'family group' is perhaps the one most commonly used. I will use it here if only because it takes an accepted social unit and places it within an educational setting. Every family is composed of people of different ages, expectations, skills, experience, understanding, gifts and abilities. To the family each person brings his own qualities, from it he draws support.

The family-grouped class is based upon a similar ideal. Where a school is organized in this way, each class will bridge several school years. Five, six and seven year olds might be found in one class, or seven, eight and nine year olds, or nine, ten and eleven year olds. The actual division will be determined by the teaching staff and it is impossible to define the age-spreads in any but the most general terms. Let me, however, first clear away a misconception before outlining the reasons for this approach being introduced.

The term 'family' should never be regarded in its actual sense – all the Smith children irrespective of age are not dumped together to be taught with all the Browns and all the Richardsons. Of course, in some schools children from the same home will be found together in the same family-grouped classroom. In other schools there is an unwritten rule never to put children together from the same family unless parents so request it.

The educational basis for family-grouped teaching stems from two broad principles – one intellectual, one social. Each child is different. Each child will make discoveries about the world in which he lives at his own pace, in his own time and in his own way. This is not to say that we should not teach certain basic facts and expect that these facts should be acquired at a particular stage in a child's development. However the rote learning of prescribed material does not imply that understanding has taken place, nor does it mean that while we are manfully teaching one thing the child is not consciously and wilfully or subconsciously and accidentally learning something quite different. I can vividly remember learning to decline the French verb 'aimer' without the faintest idea of what ending I would use in the sentences my teacher laboriously wrote on the blackboard, and I can equally well remember having their significance revealed a year later when I began Latin. For twelve months my French had been disastrous through no fault of my own. I had learned what I had been told to learn, I had understood nothing – for I had built up my own pattern for verb use, which though reasonable on purely intuitive grounds was quite unrelated to French as spoken in France. Applying my experience to a five or six year old struggling with the mystery of reading, no amount of teaching 'b for boat' is going to allow him to apply this knowledge unless he can relate it to things within his understanding.

But the reverse also applies. There were, no doubt, boys in my class at school for whom French presented no difficulties, who were bored by the whole slow ritual of 'Marcel and Denise' as they trudged from page to page of our primer. These boys would have been more excited and learned far more effectively from direct language experience supported by periodic dips into current issues of *Le Monde*.

But surely this difference in the pace of acquiring, developing and using skills does not only apply to the adolescent or the adult. It applies to every child from the moment of birth. There are some babies who seem to have learned to walk without even having had to crawl, there are others who have learned to speak so easily that their language development needs little adult help. At the same time there are children who, it seems, are only too prepared to remain immobile and silent.

Family grouping is an educational acknowledgement of human behaviour and learning patterns. Some five year olds will come to school with quite advanced reading skills, with knowledge of number; others will come with nothing. Some five year olds will have the language level we might expect of a child two years older; others will come to school with a language level so rudimentary that communication of any sort is difficult, if not impossible, to achieve. Some children, uninfluenced by home, will suddenly discover that they have a special gift in the visual arts; others that they are charismatic leaders and can organize their colleagues; others will find that numbers are so interesting that school days without mathematics are empty and without challenge.

Therefore if it is accepted that the pace of learning is different for each child, a family-grouped organization is more likely to meet each child's need on an individual level. A range of mathematical experiences, where the bright alert six year old is working alongside a less confident eight year old is demeaning for neither child if each is being extended by the activity. An eight year old who has not mastered phonics is less likely to feel ill at ease when working with younger children on basic language activities if – though basic – such activities are an accepted part of the school day. Family grouping can be regarded, therefore, as a means of extending the advantages of mixed-ability teaching across age groups, to allow children of different aptitudes to develop at their own pace, without being circumscribed by arbitrary considerations imposed by syllabus or timetable.

There are also social advantages. The development of intellectual capacity is not the only function of a school. The classroom is also a place where social expertise is learned, where relationships are forged, formed and sustained, where the pressures of communal living are first realized. Children are social creatures who want to be accepted by their peers, by adults, by their community. Children learn much by example; their respect for others is often a reflection of their own experiences. The aim of the responsible parent and the caring teacher is to give them patterns upon which they can build, to shape by example rather than by command.

The five year old, coming into a class composed entirely of five year olds, can, of course, learn from his fellows. But since their experience of living is, in terms of years, not much greater than his, behavioural patterns within the classroom have of necessity to be dominated by the teacher. 'Now we always put our chairs under quietly. Let's all try again. No Johnny, not under Mary's place, that's silly isn't it?' might seem to be nothing more than a cheap parody at the expense of women teachers. But is it? Perhaps in the turn of phrase, in the implicit nature of the expectation you hear a faint echo of your own childhood, and feel a re-awakening of your own early reactions to schools and teachers.

The family-grouped class allows for the intellectual and social needs of children to be met and their demands fulfilled. I use the word 'demands' with reason. Parents have said to me that in general they approve of family grouping. It is seen as helping young children come to terms with school, for five year olds are admitted to a socially cohesive group, which is not undergoing the stresses which stem from admitting twenty five year olds to an institution at the same moment. Indeed the feeling of security and purpose which a mixed-age class gives to new entrants is unquestioned. The view is sometimes advanced, however, that whilst family grouping helps the younger child it may restrict the progress of the oldest children in the group. 'It's all very well providing an environment for the fives and sixes,' one mother said to me, 'but what about the seven year olds. Isn't their work held back by the younger ones?'

To criticize family grouping in this way is understandable. But the observation is, in my opinion, ill-founded. It assumes that the teacher is not as concerned with the pace of work and the intellectual development of her older children as she is with her younger ones. It assumes that individual work, which is just as challenging for a child as it would be in a streamed year-based class, is not taking place. It also assumes that 'pace' invariably describes slow, dreamy, leisurely movement and never movement which is rapid, sharp and incisive.

Much depends, in any teaching situation, on the expectation of the teacher and of the other adults in the child's world. In any class (whether family grouped or tightly streamed), where the expectations are low the response from the child will be low. If the role of the older child is seen by the teacher as that of a 'monitor' whose main task is to help his younger classmates, then there will be a decline in real achievement. But then the failings of professionals don't just occur in teaching, or in teaching younger children, or when teachers use less traditional methods. Failure is more often the result of misunderstanding, incompetence or plain ignorance of what is involved. A school which operates on the basis of family-grouped classes should not be dismissed simply because of its organization, but examined on the grounds of whether it is successful or not.

Before leaving this aspect of school organization I would like to make one personal observation. Having taught in schools that were tightly streamed, in schools where the classes were year-based but de-streamed and in schools with a family-grouped organization, I much prefer the latter. Standards have not fallen because of family grouping, the same core areas of the curriculum are being covered in as much depth. Indeed I could give numerous examples of children who had made more progress in the basic skills than I would have expected because the organization allowed them to make greater use of their own particular abilities and to receive more support for their weaknesses than would have been possible in a more traditional classroom.

The most significant advantage, in my opinion, lies however in the fact that in the family-grouped class a child can regress as well as progress. By regress I mean behave on a lower social/play level than is usual. Let me illustrate this with an example. George was eight, an extremely bright child fluent in reading, writing and mathematics. Socially he was less competent – his academic brilliance had swept him quickly through that period when children experiment with sand, water, bricks and dressing-up clothes. He played chess rather than games of tag, he preferred mathematical challenges to constructional toys. His thoughts were mature, reasoned and crystal clear. He found that his own personal interests cut him off from his peers. What do you do, as a teacher, with a child of eight who observes that he believes a reduction in the money supply to £10 per head, per week, irrespective of work undertaken, would cure inflation very quickly? What do you do if such a child is your classmate? There were days when George did regress. He would play with water for hours, build with bricks, dress up, model with clay – and produce in academic terms absolutely nothing. He behaved as the office executive who returns home from a particularly tiresome day at the office and plays for several hours with his son's trains, or takes the next day off to go to the golf club to unwind.

In family-grouped classes I observe children of all ability ranges doing this and then returning (as George invariably did) refreshed to undertake some new and exacting project. Because the ages are mixed, because a range of play is acceptable and a range of materials is always available, children can lose themselves within the group when they need to do so without losing their self-respect or the respect of their peers.

In both formally streamed schools and informally family-grouped ones, subject-based teaching is sometimes practised. Here each teacher takes responsibility for a specific subject area (mathematics, English, creative arts) and becomes something of a specialist. The children in classes, year or ability groups, move between the teachers. Each teacher concentrates upon a particular area of the curriculum, and usually works in a room specially geared to the subject. The advantage of this approach is that it allows individual teachers to work in their areas of strength and professional interest, thus making sure that the maximum number of children benefit from their expertise. It also means that stock can be centrally stored and that unnecessary duplication of expensive equipment is avoided. The money saved can be spent on more sophisticated equipment or to provide additional support material for slow learners.

Thus if a mathematics laboratory is established in a junior school the money saved by buying fewer class sets of textbooks could be used for structural apparatus, electronic calculators, balances, inclined planes, a range of capacity measures and several different types of weighing machine. In the adjoining language laboratory there might be a full range of audio and visual aids as well as a variety of pre-reading and remedial-reading apparatus. Obviously this sort of specialist provision could also be made for art, music and environmental studies.

The weakness of such a structure is that it requires very tight timetabling and reduces the opportunities of teacher and child to follow through discoveries irrespective of time. It is impossible to continue a mathematical activity to its natural end with one group of children, for example, if another group is outside the door waiting to come in and begin a completely different activity. Work and equipment cannot be left out for a class to return to if the same area is to be used by everybody.

Perhaps the chief failing of such specialization is that it presents learning to children in tight subject-based units, whereas young children tend not to learn in this way. They learn across subject boundaries, relating new knowledge and skills to previous experiences irrespective of where or how these previous experiences were acquired. Should cooking, for example, be regarded as housecraft, or a means of providing basic weighing experience, or a peg on which to hang cultural customs of other lands? Could we not also regard cooking as a way of introducing shopping and home economics, or perhaps even simple science?

There is also the danger that when subject-based teaching is ruthlessly applied (as it can be), the system becomes all important, and those operating within it (child and teacher) become incidental to the method. In my opinion the primary school child needs a secure human relationship within which to work, and the fewer teachers he meets – in a professional capacity – in a day or a week, the better he fares. Indeed some of the problems which are revealed in the early years of secondary schooling – aggression, truancy, boredom – could, to some extent, be solved if the pastoral nature of the teacher's role could be re-established – and it is far easier to be seen to care and to be aware of a person's problems if you spend much of your day or your week with him. This is not to say that the specialist teacher has no part to play in the middle years of schooling, but it is arguable that the move towards subject specialism begins too early for many of our children and produces not only intellectual confusion but a welter of social and emotional problems which have to be solved at a later stage.

In this respect it is worth commenting upon the mini-school programmes in the United States. These schools were developed in decaying urban areas to meet problems of truancy, vandalism and petty crime. Each mini-school is a unit within a large school (such as a school of 200 in a school of 1,200) and it follows a programme of its own, unrelated to that followed by its parent school. Within the mini-schools I visited the teachers did not specialize to any great degree, and the children (aged between twelve and fifteen) had an emotional rather than intellectual commitment to their schools. This is all the more remarkable when it is remembered that mini-schools were developed in areas where social tension and economic decay were matters of considerable concern to the local communities where they were established; schools which had previously been regarded as irrelevant by young people who were attending them suddenly took on a new lease of life. Some of these schools had a learning programme linked to a particular industry, some included work which was based upon experiences they had had with their teachers on camping and adventure holidays. The majority of classes I observed, however, were doing the ordinary everyday things which one associates with school: reading, writing, mathematics, spelling. What was strikingly different was the children's attitudes. They wanted to be at school, they wanted to learn.

It would be foolish, however, to ignore teachers' specialisms or to refuse to admit that a brilliant language teacher might find it much more difficult to shine when teaching science or mathematics. An acceptable compromise, one that has been introduced into some schools, is co-operative teaching.

Co-operative teaching takes the most significant element of single-teacher class-based units (which is detailed knowledge of each child in her care) and builds upon it. Both parent and child can identify their 'own teacher', the one to whom they take their individual problems. But the teacher does not work only with one class, nor do the children work only with one teacher. In practice co-operative teaching usually involves two or three teachers working alongside each other, co-operating across all areas of the curriculum, so that the children find themselves working with several teachers in any one day. Although the children will probably begin and end the day with their own 'home group' teacher, at other times they may find themselves working with children who are not in their own 'home group'. These teaching groups may well be supervised by one of the other teachers in the co-operative.

The advantage of this method of working is that it allows teachers to share expertise. The teacher with a particular interest in mathematics, working with two others whose gifts lie in the graphic arts, music, poetry or literature, can give to all the children (and to her colleagues) something of her enthusiasm, supported by the knowledge that through developing and extending her interests a much greater number of children will benefit.

Sharing common working areas (for co-operative teaching often takes place in buildings where the traditional classroom boundaries have been blurred) also means that the less experienced teacher, or the one that has disciplinary problems, can be supported by colleagues.

The dispersal of children over several linked classrooms (or 'teaching areas') also means that teachers are less likely to be bound (in traditional curriculum terms) to specific age groupings. The children involved will probably spread over several primary years (for example five to eight year olds, seven to nine year olds, eight to eleven year olds) and each such group will undoubtedly embrace a wide range of abilities. This means that teaching activities can be more closely geared to the ability of children as individuals. A bright seven year old could, therefore, be encouraged to work alongside children two years his senior; a child who was having difficulty mastering reading could be placed (for some time each day) in a group of children engaged in basic reading activities. The very fact that the composition of these groups varies from activity to activity, and that each group contains a spread of ages, helps prevent children from regarding themselves either as abject failures or wild successes. The advocates of co-operative teaching argue that it is essentially an organizational structure which allows each child to be fully challenged. No longer does a child compete with his peers to obtain a class pecking order; instead he competes with himself and is helped to evaluate his own work and worth critically.

Certainly it is an appropriate method if there are teachers in a school capable of implementing it successfully. As a parent, I want to feel that my daughter's woodwind lessons match her particular level of competence, that she is not frustrated by being kept back to allow less able pupils to catch up with her. Similarly I will feel aggrieved if my son is left to struggle with his mathematics because the basic work on which progress depends has been misunderstood. The less able should not be neglected to meet the needs of the academic highfliers.

But co-operative teaching makes one other significant contribution to the development of young children. It allows them to function during any one day on a variety of levels. The child who is academically brilliant may well be emotionally immature; the child who is a slow learner may have a feeling for paint or movement. The larger the group, the easier it is for teachers working together to provide a range of activities to meet the emotional and intellectual needs of the children with whom they work.

When my present school was opened I remember expressing surprise that nine year old boys spent much of their lunch time building complex structures with infant bricks. In terms of my junior school training such an activity was not appropriate. Junior boys did not play with bricks! And yet, as I watched them, I realized that the level at which they functioned was extremely high. They talked, discussed problems, co-operated and, as a result, arrived at decisions which were acceptable to the group as a whole. Their responsibility and social cohesiveness was nothing short of remarkable. When analysing why they felt they could play in this way, I discovered that the bricks were kept in a common shared area. The place 'was a place where bricks were' – it was, therefore, reasonable for these older lads to use them. 'No one would notice we were big,' Martin explained to me. 'In my other school bricks were for infants and we'd have looked silly playing with them.' And then, as if to justify himself, he added, 'I never had bricks when I was little and we live in a flat.'

The fact that a well-structured and adequately furnished co-operative teaching area can contain a range of materials means that the academic, social and emotional extremes of the children for whom it is catering can be met. Moreover the teacher can provide these materials without attempting to define clearly which children will use them. Daniel's teacher, for example, was prepared for his rapid advance in mathematics. He knew all the basic number bonds ($6 + 7 = 13$ etc.) before he was five. He could read and he was fascinated with words. I'm not sure, however, whether she was prepared for the long hours he spent playing with sand and water, painting and picture making with fabric scraps and junk. For several years Daniel seemed to be saying, 'I can do all the things appropriate to my age. I'm seven. I can read like a twelve year old, recite square numbers by heart, define a square, a hexagon and a triangle. Let me do the things I also need to do as a child before it's too late.' It is perhaps appropriate to conclude this example by observing that when Daniel had worked through his period of 'catching up', he was still far ahead, academically, of many of his fellows.

The realization that a curriculum which accepted human

differences as well as the similarity of their needs has prompted educationalists to vary the structure of the working day. The development of open-plan schools, for example, has been described by some of its critics as a device for saving money. 'If a school is built like a barn, with few internal dividing walls and no doors, it will be cheaper.' This is attributing political overtones to changes which, in the first instant, were purely educational ones.

Open-plan schools, many of which were built in the sixties and early seventies, were a reflection of how teachers, psychologists and architects saw children using space. A curriculum freed from the barriers imposed by subject teaching needed a more fluid environment in which to flourish. If teachers and children were sharing common areas, these areas should flow one into another.

If co-operative teaching is being practised with family-grouped classes, then the building should reflect this. A group of three teachers working with ninety children will not make the same demands upon a building as three teachers each working with her own class of thirty children. Sometimes there might be an activity (like a film) which will enable one teacher to be responsible for sixty children, while one colleague works with twenty-five children and her other colleague with only five.

In these circumstances the school building takes on quite a different image. There are home bases for such things as stories, registration and discussion time, but the general 'feel' of the school is utterly unlike that which most adults remember from their own childhood.

Herein lies the danger; for a method which we, as parents and teachers, have not directly experienced in education can easily become threatening – even though the fact that open-plan schools have areas designated for music, mathematics and visual aids, a library and a language centre might go some way to reassure us. Somehow there is a feeling of diffuseness, a lack of clarity and identifiable objectives.

It is probably because open-plan buildings were too quickly developed in some areas that the late seventies have seen yet another change in direction. The 'modified open-plan' incorporates both open, shared teaching spaces and quiet withdrawal rooms. It acknowledges something which all who work with children have always known – that for some activities, such as dance, large communal spaces are required whilst for others, such as poetry reading, a more intimate atmosphere is necessary. Further, it accepts the fact that one space cannot meet the functional demands of every activity. It is sensible to provide carpeted areas for children to sit on, but foolish to do so if they are expected to use clay there as well. Similarly it is appropriate to put out percussion instruments for children to use, but if they are continually being played in a barn-like building they will distract those children who are engaged in quieter, more academic occupations.

It is against this background of change in teaching style (and the resulting change in the pattern of the school day) that the arguments of the educational traditionalists must be considered.

The Black Papers on education (the first of which was published in the late sixties) were an attempt to alert the general public to the changes which had been occurring in education since the end of the war. These papers – which called for a return to traditional teaching methods in both primary and secondary schools – were edited by Dr Rhodes Boyson (a former teacher and now a Conservative MP) and Professor Cox (of Manchester University). The papers were a motley collection of articles written by educationalists representing a variety of disciplines. Sadly they were ill-argued and smacked of elitism. Even the most recent paper (1977) was criticized by the most conservative of educationalists as having nothing to offer for the future, being more a wail for a past long dead than a call for a better tomorrow.

But the Black Papers have served a very useful purpose. They have encouraged greater thought on the aims, purpose and direction of our schools. They have challenged current practice. They have demanded – albeit stridently – that teachers should be made more accountable to parents, that new approaches to teaching and changes in the curriculum should not be made without reasonable consultation with all who have an interest in the child.

What the Black Papers have singularly failed to do is to offer an alternative to parents, to teachers, to education authorities. A return to more traditional methods, class-based teaching, to a clearly defined curriculum with internal and external evaluation by marks and grades, is likely to meet young people's needs no more now than it did forty years ago (when the majority of the child population left school at fourteen and the fortunate few went on to sit the General Schools Certificate).

Against all this ferment of change one thing must be kept in mind: recent research (*Teaching Styles and Pupil Progress* by Neville Bennet, Open Books, 1976) suggests that some 16 per cent of our primary schools are 'progressive' (that is, using some or all of the variants I have described above). If this figure is an accurate one, then it must be obvious that such changes as have occurred in primary education are local rather than national. The variety of schools, and the variety of approach of each school, is both the strength and the weakness of the English system. Although some local authorities manage, through charismatic leadership and a dedicated teaching force, to stamp a recognizable pattern upon the schools they administer (like the West Riding under Alec Clegg and Oxfordshire County under Edith Moorhouse), such uniformity is the exception rather than the rule.

As parents or teachers, perhaps all that we can say of a school is that it fits this or that general pattern, for to attempt to define the traditional English primary school is, as I have suggested, virtually impossible.

3 *Approaches to Learning*

When attempting to describe the curriculum of the primary school, a writer is faced with an almost insoluble problem. As I have already implied, there is no such thing as a typical primary school. Each individual school has its own curriculum and the task of each head is to ensure that this curriculum (which he and his colleagues have designed) is taught in such a way as to maintain the continuity of a child's learning throughout his time in the school. Each school also tries to ensure that the level of attainment it achieves in basic subjects (reading, writing, number) is appropriate to the age groups for which it is catering. This is an essential consideration in an age when changes in the pattern of employment have introduced a flexibility into the life style of the parents of young children. In the course of one academic year many thousands of children move from one primary school to another. For transfers to be as efficiently effected as these are (and there is little evidence of public disquiet in this area) would suggest that there already exists a core curriculum which is common to the majority of schools in the country.

Superficially it might appear that these two elements (staff freedom and a core or agreed curriculum) are in conflict. This is not the case. Disagreements within the teaching profession have not centred so much on the content of the curriculum as on the methods employed in our schools. This debate has concentrated upon the professional role of the teacher and it has been conducted, in the main, by the teachers themselves. Whenever outside bodies (government, employers, parent associations) chose to intervene or to comment, the professional bodies expressed concern at the threat to the freedom which teachers had so long enjoyed.

Even this vision of professional freedom, however, is something of a mirage. Heads and senior members of their staff can make changes in the pattern of the school day, alter the direction of the curriculum by emphasizing one area rather than another or by actively supporting and encouraging a particular project. But all schools are subject to a variety of external pressures and it is these as much as professional attitudes which will encourage change or mitigate against it.

Let me illustrate this with some examples. Change will be most obviously expected when a headteacher retires or moves to another post, and all who are involved with the school look to the future with anxiety, relief or expectation. Although a change of headteacher will undoubtedly affect the way a school is organized, changes in the senior staff of a school probably have an even greater impact. A new headteacher is unlikely to be able to alter the traditions and practice of a school in the face of fierce opposition from long-established teachers; a headteacher of considerable experience may be unable to continue to develop the curriculum of a school in a particular way if senior teachers implementing it are promoted, or even to introduce experimental methods of working if the majority of his staff are new to teaching. Staff stability is an important consideration when examining the practice of a school. The spoken ideals of the headteacher and his staff might not appear to be in tune with what is actually happening in the school. Without other evidence this situation should not be taken, *per se*, as an indication of professional dishonesty but rather as an acceptance of what can best be accomplished with the resources (human and physical) that are available. In the school in which I work, for example, I have tried to encourage a free exchange of ideas, to develop ways of using an open-plan school effectively, to involve parents and teachers in the learning processes that the children undergo. These are ideals; whether they succeed or fail during any one school year depends as much on the teachers that are working in the school (and whom I may not have appointed*)

* A proportion of the teaching staff of any school are appointed by the local education authority and not by the headteacher and the school governors.

as on my ability to spell out to them my requirements and expectations.

Another factor which may cause the curriculum to undergo change is external to the school – the pupils attending it. The social composition of an area may alter, bringing a subtle but profound change in what parents expect of the school. For example an inner city district becomes fashionable, house prices rise and educated, articulate 'professional' parents descend upon a school which had hitherto concerned itself with less well-endowed members of society. In this example, changes in the school will not simply reflect staff decisions but also the specific demands the children themselves will make of their teachers. There is no point in concentrating upon a reading scheme and a set of primers if the majority of the children can read before they come to school.

This sort of change is one of which I have some personal experience. The school I teach in is made up of children from almost every social background. For some of the children, the county primary school acts as a bridge between the nursery years and the preparatory and public school which is to come. For many others the schooling which the staff provide is the only schooling that can be made available to them, since their parents are unable to buy an alternative. The two groups exist happily together, yet I am aware that the needs and aspirations of both are often quite different. Such moments of insight as I have had, however, indicate how difficult it can be to resolve the underlying tensions. The case of Mary illustrates this point. She was ten years old and one of five children. Her mother's boy friend, just released from prison, was given to violent rages. In one of these he had assaulted Mary, stabbed her sister and battered her mother. The day following this outburst, Mary came to school in a hysterical state. I devoted much of the day to find ways of helping Mary and her mother. In the late afternoon, however, another mother sought my advice on secondary education. She had two children, Peter and Sarah, who were aged nine and seven, and felt that they should attend a private school when they reached the age of eleven. This interview was interrupted by Mary who burst in upon us, crying uncontrollably. As I tried to comfort her I was surprised to hear Peter's mother observe, 'Children from poor homes take so much time. We really ought to rethink our priorities. After all the future of the country depends upon how well we educate those children who will benefit from education.' If this attitude is typical (and I hope it is not) is it possible to adopt a curriculum which will meet the needs of all the children in our school? Mary looked to school for love, affection and security: Peter and Sarah looked to it for skills in number, for learning techniques, for methods of recording facts and findings. The needs of these children were not irreconcilable. Mary, Peter and Sarah needed love and skills. The expectancy of their two mothers, however, was quite different. For one school was a place of refuge, for the other a place to take specific problems: 'I want this for my child. He will need to pass these examinations. What can you and your teachers do to see that he does so?'

Ethnic changes in the local population will also have an effect upon curriculum content. In some inner city areas there has been a considerable change in the character of the population. Indigenous, English-speaking Christians have been replaced by newcomers for whom English is a second language and Christianity an alien creed. For a school serving such an area to continue to teach a traditional curriculum would be foolhardy, for new situations demand new solutions.

If the curriculum of a particular school must be examined against a background of slow, subtle and continuous change it must also be somehow set within the broad framework of accepted practice. But the freedom that teachers have to determine the methods they employ makes 'accepted practice' very difficult to define.

In the past ten years my interest in creative work with young children has taken me into schools in every part of the British Isles and to British schools across the world. This experience has served to confirm the fact that no two schools are alike.

One school I visited recently, for example, had all the hallmarks of traditional methods firmly applied. The children were tightly marshalled in the playground before they were allowed into the building; as they moved along the corridors and stairways their movement was controlled by prefects. The day opened with registration and an assembly which was presided over by the headteacher. The assembly over, a senior member of staff stepped forward to review the week's scores in the inter-house competition. The children then retired, class by class, in silence to their rooms.

Within each classroom, however, the atmosphere was relaxed. The children worked confidently on a variety of assignments and the 'style' employed by the teaching staff was impossible to classify. This was certainly not a 'formal' school in the accepted sense of the word. Blackboards were used, but sparingly; the classes were year-based, but unstreamed; there was a 'nuture' group for the small number of difficult emotionally disturbed children who could not cope with school life.

The headteacher described himself as a traditionalist. He liked a 'tidy school', which he compared to a 'tidy ship'. He obviously knew his parents, knew his children and enjoyed an excellent relationship with his staff. He prepared, with staff help, a syllabus for each year group in each subject area. There was a timetable and the timetable was followed with few deviations throughout the year.

As a visitor I was impressed by the way the children concentrated upon the work they were doing, by the enthusiasm they showed as they talked about their paintings, writings and models. Indeed the arts seemed to flourish, with more time being given to dance, drama, music and pottery than I have found in many schools where the head considered himself 'a liberal'.

Another school, in a quietly rural part of England, was also presented to me as following a formal programme, but this was something of an understatement. It was unmistakably grey. The organization had certain similarities to the school I have described above. The classes were unstreamed and year based, and there was a house system. There the similarities end. The classrooms, with desks arranged in rows, were as uninspiring as much of the teaching. The walls, decorated with a scruffy selection of paintings and pictures from newspapers and magazines, did nothing to give children a vision of the worth of their work. The headteacher had little time for modern methods, or for 'window dressing' (which is how he seemed to view all art-based subjects). The overall impression I gained was of a place where children and their interests and gifts were debased. The level of boredom, of both teachers and children, was high. The school day was something to get through as best one could before the real business of living began.

I remember comparing this school with one I visited in the West Riding of Yorkshire. The school itself was housed in a scruffy building in the centre of a small mining village. To enter the building, however, was to enter another world, a world full of light and colour. It is true that its interior had been refurbished; the glass partitions which once divided the classrooms had been taken away and replaced by low movable screens. The space (there were no classrooms as such) was filled with displays of children's work. There were paintings, poetry and prose writings, graphs and charts, and 'museum areas' which contained exhibitions of mining equipment and local animal life. A rabbit, running free, was curiously nibbling the edge of a piece of curtaining. There were children working together in small purposeful groups. The noise level was extremely low. There was no obvious adult presence. I asked a member of the teaching staff to describe her role. She said that she was 'an enabler', a person who enabled children to learn by providing all the facilities they needed for doing so. 'If they need to learn techniques like holding a pen or making a letter "a" I teach it. If they need extra love and affection I give it and as they need security and order, I see they have that too.'

The organization of the school was so fluid as to be virtually undefinable. There was no set syllabus, few textbooks, little evidence of formal teaching. Yet the children were knowledge-able, could read and computate and the majority of them seemed to have mastered italic handwriting. There was no organized parent-teacher association, but ample evidence of the many ways in which parents were involved in school life; there was no school football team but, as the head explained, 'we do have a good orchestra'.

My final example is drawn from the home counties. The school, purpose-built and beautifully furnished, is, one might imagine, a place in which modern methods will really flourish. A short tour of the building is enough to depress the most enthusiastic advocate of curriculum innovation. The children, family-grouped and informally seated, look bored and somewhat sullen. The environment might be right for children, but no one has shown them how to use it. There are displays, but they look a bit battered, there is a library, but the books have been ill cared for, there are Wendy houses and giant climbing frames, but these, like much of the school, have become a tatty symbol of a method which the teachers never seem quite to have mastered or understood.

The excuses (or rather the explanations) which were advanced for this state of things were the ones most often advanced to explain away professional failure. The children were from a slum rehousing development, there was a high incidence of one-parent families, the teaching staff were young and inexperienced and 'kept leaving', and those that remained just didn't understand how to use the building.

For all its bright paintwork and expensive furnishings this too was a grey school, a place lacking in direction and purpose, an institution which did little to introduce even a semblance of order into young lives which had already experienced more than their fair share of upheaval and unrest.

It was a school that left me feeling very uncomfortable. It was no worse a school than the indifferent formal school I have described in an earlier paragraph, and yet, because the frustrations of the children were more obvious, I felt more alarmed. Was this because silent, depressed children are less of a threat to us as adults? Is that why we find the media less critical of poor 'formal' schools than poor 'informal' ones?

To say that the two examples of successful schools represent the best of English primary method might, at first glance, seem unlikely; on reflection initial doubts would probably be replaced by sheer disbelief. How can schools within one state system be so different in their approach to the curriculum, so different in their teaching style? As I shall indicate in chapters which follow, these differences may be traced back to the way in which education became the responsibility of government in the last half of the nineteenth century, to sectarian interests and to the traditional spirit of compromise which characterizes British public life.

And yet, despite the superficial differences in my two examples, strong basic similarities remain. The curriculum – in one school defined and detailed, in the second unwritten and open-ended – has a common central core. The need for children to speak, read and write their mother tongue fluently was emphasized by both teaching staffs, the importance of an understanding of basic number recognized, and courses were provided in religious studies, history, geography, music, science, physical education, homecraft and the arts. At 11 + the ground covered might well prove to be virtually identical. It is the manner in which it is covered that distinguishes one school from the other.

Variations in teaching style are not only to be found between different schools. There are often considerable variations within each school. In one school in which I worked the children began each day with a free period which was devoted to individual project work, model-making, painting, pottery, drama and creative writing. After the mid-morning break (at 10.30 am) the regime became much more formal with the teachers following a tightly structured curriculum, largely textbook-based, until 3.30 pm. The last part of the afternoon was spent on class planning with the children, determining the range and direction of the 'free' activities that they would undertake the following morning.

Thus the casual visitor would have found it difficult to place the school in any particular educational grouping. Were he to visit it at 10.00 am he would certainly have felt that he were watching a 'free school' in action; a visit made an hour later would have given the overriding impression of traditionalism. The longer I worked in this school the more I became aware that it was possible to live and work quite successfully in an institution where compromise underlay all that took place. The assemblies, for example, were prepared by the children but presided over by the headteacher and the two senior pupils (head boy and head girl). There was no academic competition within the school. All the leavers received a prize and class prizes were given to the children who were remaining. These class prizes were subsequently placed in the school library to be shared by all. Fierce competition, however, was encouraged on the games field. The school entered local leagues for netball, rounders, football and cricket as well as a number of swimming galas. Team games were presented to the children as a way of learning about life – that playing was more important than winning, that to lose well was as much a mark of distinction as winning graciously. But in practice the desire to defeat other schools played a much more significant part than anyone was prepared to admit.

Looking back at this school, in which I spent four reasonably successful and happy years, I realize that the children were constantly expected to cope with extremes – freedom of choice and denial of choice; belief in the individual's place in a society which met his needs and almost blind acceptance of a society where the individual came second to the team, the house, the school; an acceptance of competition while rejecting its value as a driving force in the life of the community or of the individuals within it.

On leaving the school I moved to another where the headteacher believed in an ordered curriculum, streamed classes, a defined timetable, prize days, monitors, craft classes for children over the age of nine (the boys taking bookcraft, the girls needlecraft), a school in which corporal punishment was not uncommon. On the surface there was an ordered hierarchy. Yet this particular headteacher believed that a school could only be successful if he allowed many of his inbuilt structures to be ignored by teachers who felt that they had more appropriate ways of meeting the needs of their classes than those he had suggested. Within this school there were classes which were organized in an informal way (grouped desks, rich displays, free movement within the rooms and the surrounding area). At the same time there were classes which were entirely teacher-dominated, where the headteacher's recommended curriculum was followed without question. As in my previous example, it would have been impossible to place this school as representative of a particular educational grouping. Some aspects of its life and methods of working could be described as enlightened; others had more in common with the conservative thinking of the 1920s than the freer approaches that characterized the 1960s.

In both these schools the children coped with the uneven educational practice that they were offered. But is this so surprising? Most adults, looking back on their own school days, can remember which teachers they respected and which they ignored, which teachers fired them with enthusiasm and which bored them to tears, which were liberal in their attitudes and which were dogmatic, unsympathetic and downright cruel. Young children have the facility to sum up adults very quickly and learn to cope with the particular idiosyncrasies (of subject presentation and method) of the teachers with whom they share the school building.

In the light of this, it might be argued that it would be better if each school did have a clearly defined philosophy. Surely teaching and learning would be more effective if clarity of purpose and the direction and content of the curriculum were first defined and then implemented? Certain educationalists and politicians would go even further and suggest that if an agreement on national standards and teaching methods could be reached then children need never be faced with the variety of teaching styles and diversity of curriculum content that has characterized English primary schools since the end of the Second World War.

This, however, is to over-simplify the process of teaching, to reduce the rapport which exists between the gifted teacher and her class to the level of fact giver. The way to develop and extend children is not by narrowing options but by keeping them open so that whatever method is thought to be most suitable can be applied when it is appropriate. This belief is common to all teachers who practise child-centred education, for child-centred education is not based upon an idealist's desire to give children freedom. In the school where children are really respected the parameters within which the children move are clearly defined. Children are not given more freedom than they can manage, nor are they given less. The successful teacher is continually redefining the boundaries within which her children work, confirming by approval the good things they do, expressing concern when individual behaviour falls below that which is expected.

Thus emphasis is placed on the positive contributions which each child makes to the school community: children are not placed in straitjackets (as they were in my childhood) to prevent them from behaving in any way, for good or ill, outside the pattern defined by the school.

The contemporary primary school is seeking to give children the opportunity to develop their own particular gifts. By making the programme purposeful the disciplines imposed (and thereby acquired by the children) are largely self-taught. Directly a person enters a community whether a scout group, a youth club, or a school, limitations are imposed upon his actions. These limitations are not all imposed by adults. Many will stem from the relationships he makes within the group and decisions which the group makes about common objectives. If, for example, a class of nine year olds decide to build a large model castle which will take up most of the spare space in the classroom, those children who would have preferred to build a Viking ship or a space rocket will have to contain their enthusiasm to do so and contribute to the common purpose. Mutual regard for others and respect for differing viewpoints is at the root of the freedoms that we enjoy in our society. The more young people become socially disciplined and are shown the relevance of patience, tolerance and co-operation in their everyday lives, the fewer rules we will need to impose. This point was made to me quite dramatically by a social worker in the Bronx, New York. Looking across a wasteland of urban decay she observed, 'It's no good teaching people about social living if they aren't allowed to live socially. It's the same with reading,' she went on. 'What's the point of teaching people to read if you don't show them how to read with discretion?'

In the situation I have described the classroom teacher is not opting out and giving children freedoms they cannot use. She will be providing them with materials which will need to be worked, tools which will only function if handled correctly, ideas which will challenge, situations (like drama) which demand considerable poise and self-control. Freedom in these terms should not be regarded as the antithesis of control. The teacher is still exercising control by determining how much freedom is allowed to an individual, a group, a class. Just as the wise parent increases the amount of freedom a child is allowed as he moves from babyhood through childhood to adolescence, so does the caring teacher. As parents we should define at an early stage what sort of behaviour we will tolerate and the sorts of response we expect to the needs and wellbeing of others. Many of the crises of adolescence could be avoided, I am sure, if this very elementary course of action were taken. Suddenly to become authoritarian with a teenage girl, for example, about the hours she comes home when you have never bothered about the times she kept as a smaller child is surely quite unreasonable. Similarly, for a teacher to accept poor work or intolerant behaviour simply by ignoring it is to perform a disservice to the child. The strength of the contemporary primary school is that teachers are less desk-bound, and are more aware that growth is a paradox of continuation and creation. We build upon what has gone before, we create new things upon ideals, attitudes and skills that were first awoken by others. Classes are no longer seen as personal projections of individual teachers, but as individual children to whom everyone in the school society (teachers, ancillaries, parents, children) has something to give.

The difficulties in considering discipline in these terms stem in the main from our own childhood experiences in school. We probably remember school as a place where firm control was imposed by the headteacher, supported by staff and prefects. As an approach (and it is an approach still followed in many parts of the world) it did not seem particularly inefficient. The bright children learned, those of middle ability coped, the slow children were contained. Expectations (that school would be a fairly dull, uneventful grind) were fulfilled. It is true, of course, that in such a setting discipline is likely to appear, superficially, to be better. If children can go to the library (or to the toilet) only when told to do so, if being imprisoned behind a desk is what learning is about, if an educated child is one who manages to retain a vast number of facts, then the methods practised by our Victorian grandparents have much to commend them.

But learning is also about living, and living involves making mistakes as well as enjoying success. Perhaps the greatest and most significant contribution that primary school practice has made to our understanding of children is that it has given children the opportunity to learn about themselves and to appreciate the needs and anxieties of others. In the process teachers have come to realize that for all our sophistication we have largely ignored the potential of the children with whom they work.

Variety between schools and even between classrooms in the same school, subtle variations of emphasis on curriculum matters, differences in our attitudes to freedom and discipline, the views we hold on the purpose of early schooling, the value we place on happiness and self-fulfilment, all conspire to make it virtually impossible for me to define in one tight phrase the typical English primary school. The schools I visit, the schools I read about, the schools my own children have attended, the school I work in, have all been hybrids, neither freely informal nor tightly disciplined and rigid.

The problem of understanding the nature of primary education has not been made easier by the media or by politicians who see in education a way of promoting their particular vision of the nature of contemporary society. The primary school is not a battleground in which the political left confront the political right, in which traditionalists fight a rearguard action against progressives, in which heady views of freedom are contrasted with order, in which authoritarian paternalism is offered as the alternative to soft, sentimental child-centredness.

Rather than become lost in the somewhat specious claims of either camp, it is necessary to accept that neither approach will meet all that a child needs throughout his school life. If life is a compromise, so is education, for the aim of education is to help children cope with their life – both in the immediate business of living and in a future that we (their parents and their teachers) will not be around to share.

Our evaluation of primary schools and their curriculum must be based upon effectiveness in explaining the world to our children, in helping them to use the resources which are available to develop their own skills and innate abilities, and in developing in them a sensitivity to the needs and aspirations of others. Schools should not be condemned simply because of their style of working; they must be assessed on whether learning is seen to take place. It has been said, and in my opinion rightly so, that the informal school expects more of its teachers and its pupils than its formal counterpart. It may well be that we have not yet developed sufficient skills in teacher training to contemplate an immediate widespread extension of less formal methods. It could also be argued that informal methods need to be introduced even more slowly than they have been hitherto, since to teach informally with success requires a sophistication that our teaching force does not possess. But to advance these arguments as the basis for a return to rote learning is foolish. No society should reject innovatory methods, in any sphere of human activity, simply because everybody cannot apply them with equal success.

4 Past into Present

The year 1870 was significant in the history of education in England. It marked the first real attempt by government to ensure that elementary education would be available for all. Although Forster's Education Act (as it came to be known) is rightly regarded as a milestone in educational development, earlier administrations had authorized the expenditure of public money on schools and schooling.

Schools had existed in England long before 1870. Some had been established in the sixteenth, seventeenth and eighteenth centuries by the charitably minded rich to help educate the children of the deserving poor. Although initially founded as schools for the public they gradually changed their role as the value of their endowments fell, forcing them to take fee payers to meet their day-to-day expenses. (This explains the fact that 'public' in an educational sense means 'private', an added confusion for the foreign reader.)

The eighteenth century had also seen the development of charity schools. These were day schools established by the Society for the Propagation of the Gospel at which the children of the poor could learn to read and write and study the Bible. A charge of between fourpence and ninepence a week was made, but this of itself placed even this rudimentary education beyond the reach of many of the people that the charity schools had been designed to help.

Then there were the private schools – schools which have been described by Charles Dickens in *Nicholas Nickleby* and *Hard Times*. Dickens visited one such school (Bowes Academy, County Durham) in February 1838. His experiences prompted him to write the following advertisement into *Nicholas Nickleby* which Nicholas himself answered:

'Education. At Mr Wackford Squeers' Academy, Dotheboys

Hall, at the delightful village of Dotheboys near Greta Bridge in Yorkshire. Youths are boarded, clothed, booked, furnished with pocket money, provided with all necessaries, instructed in all languages living and dead, mathematics, orthography, geometry, astronomy, trigonometry, the use of the globes, algebra, single stick (if required), writing, arithmetic, fortification, and every branch of classical literature. Terms – twenty guineas per annum. No extras, no vacations, and diet unparelleled. Mr Squeers is in town and attends daily, from one till four, at the Saracen's Head, Snow Hill.

N.B. An able assistant wanted. Annual salary £5. A Master of Arts would be preferred.'

Not all private schools were as bad as those condemned by Dickens, but similar advertisements to that shown here filled the columns of the London *Times* in the 1830s and 1840s, which would suggest that Dickens was commenting upon school life as he saw it and as it really was. Of course, there were gentler establishments. The dame schools (so called because they were run by a schoolmistress) gave a modicum of learning to children who attended them. Miss Wackles, whose establishment appears in the *Old Curiosity Shop*, is something of a caricature. The standard of reading and writing achieved by the pupils, however, *was* often very low, a reflection of the poor education the Dame herself had enjoyed.

'This spot was at Chelsea, for there Miss Sophia Wackles resided with her widowed mother and two sisters, in conjunction with whom she maintained a very small day-school for young ladies of proportionate dimensions; which was made known to the neighbourhood by an oval board over the front first-floor window, whereupon the words, "Ladies' Seminary". The several duties of instruction in this establishment were thus discharged: English grammar, composition, geography, and the use of the dumb-bells, by Miss Melissa Wackles; writing, arithmetic, dancing, music, and general fascination, by Miss Sophy Wackles; the art of needlework, marking and samplery, by Miss Jane Wackles; corporal punishment, fasting, and other tortures and terrors, by Mrs Wackles ... an excellent but rather venemous lady of threescore.'

The schools mentioned so far – public, private, charity and dame – provided regular daily education (usually for a fee). They touched but a small proportion of the population. The beginning of the nineteenth century was marked by a growing interest in providing education (particularly reading, writing and Bible study) for the children of the 'lower classes'. In the 1780s Robert Raikes, for example, pioneered the 'Sunday School' movement. Classes met for a few hours each Sunday. However enthusiastic the teaching, little could be achieved in so short a time. Dr Kay Shuttleworth, who founded Battersea Training College in 1840, wrote a number of occasional papers on education. One includes an interview with a Mr Thomas Cooper, who said of his teacher, Old Gatty, and his schooldays in the early 1800s: 'Old Gatty was an expert and laborious teacher of the art of reading and spelling and could soon read the 10th Chapter of Nehemiah with all its hard names like the parson in church and could spell wondrously.'

The beginning of the nineteenth century also saw the establishment of two bodies which were to have a profound influence on educational development for the next hundred years. In 1811 Andrew Bell, a priest of the Church of England, became agent consultant of The National Society for Promoting the Education of the Poor in the Principles of the Established Church.

The National Society was the response of the Anglican Church to the work of Joseph Lancaster. Lancaster, a Quaker, had founded the Royal Lancastrian Institution * in 1808 to bring education to the 'labouring' classes. In this he had received considerable support from members of the British royal family and it was this patronage of a non-conformist organization which, more than any other single factor, prompted the Anglican Church to devote so much of its resources to education in the decades which were to follow.

Both Bell and Lancaster employed the monitorial system in their schools. The master taught a group of older children

* In 1814 this became the British and Foreign Schools' Society.

(monitors) who then taught the same lesson to a group of younger children. The curriculum followed by these schools was narrow, although gardening and needlecraft were added to the usual diet of reading, writing, arithmetic and religion.

The Churches, however, could not cope with the demands that an ever-increasing population made upon their schools. In 1833 the state intervened, not to take over education but to encourage the two Church societies to continue in their commitment. Education was a useful activity to encourage. At the very least it was a sop to the political unrest and popular discontent! So in 1833 a grant of £20,000 was made from public funds to assist with school buildings where no schools existed. As was to be expected much of the money found its way to the more prosperous areas of the country, for it was given to those communities who could provide a site, meet the running costs and were prepared to pay half the actual building expenses. Financial commitment was followed by direct government involvement. In 1839 the Education Committee of the Privy Council was established, two inspectors of education were appointed and in 1846 a teacher training programme was introduced.

The period 1840–60 probably marks the high point of Church involvement in education. By 1860 there were some 22,500 day schools in the country – 19,500 of them controlled by the Church of England. We should not think, however, that the existence of schools meant that children were being taught.* 80 per cent of the children who attended left before they reached the age of twelve and of these 70 per cent mastered neither reading nor writing.

No government has ever liked authorizing expenditure on an inefficient service. The inevitable inquiry followed. Headed by Lord Newcastle it recommended that 'sound and cheap' education should be provided for 'all classes of people'. A novel method was introduced to ensure that standards would rise

*E. J. Hobsbawm, in *The Age of Revolution* (Weidenfeld & Nicolson, 1962), estimates that in the 1830s between 45 per cent and 50 per cent of the adult population in England were illiterate.

– payment by results. Each school was given a grant of twelve shillings a year for each pupil. Four shillings was awarded for attendance and eight shillings for the child's performance on tests. Each year an inspector arrived to test the children in reading, writing and arithmetic. On passing the test children were moved into the next standard.

This system lasted for thirty years. It achieved little, for teachers quickly learned to prepare children to repeat parrot-like the answers to 'test' questions. The curriculum was restricted in the process, the quality of teaching fell.

It is against this background of Church commitment and state intervention that Forster's Education Act must be set. It enabled schools to be built in areas where none had hitherto existed. The Church societies were to be encouraged to build additional schools, but if the societies did not respond School Boards were to be established. The Boards would be financed from central government and from local rates. Education, non-denominational, would be provided for all children between the ages of five and ten. At this stage education was not free (parents had to pay up to ninepence a week according to their means), nor was it compulsory. In this way the elementary school – from which the modern primary school has grown – was born.

Until the Forster Act the central government had played its part in providing money for education. The Act meant that it would henceforward share this responsibility with local authorities (a situation which still obtains today). The years which followed saw many significant changes. Attendance was made compulsory, the leaving age raised to thirteen and a Board of Education established. In 1902 the School Boards were swept away and County Councils * given the responsibility for establishing and running schools within their boundaries and given the further task of supplying, and permission to train, teachers to man them. The state also assumed responsibility for voluntary schools.

This organizational pattern has continued to the present day,

* In urban areas county borough councils had this responsibility.

with local authorities having responsibility for the day-to-day running of schools within a framework established by central government. It must be emphasized, however, that many of the most fundamental decisions are made at local rather than at national level. Central government may lay down guidelines for secondary education but the local authority (which may be of a different political persuasion from the central government) enjoys considerable autonomy when determining how best to apply them within its own area. For example, the nature of secondary schools and the method of transfer to them from primary and middle schools is determined at local level. Parents do have the right to appeal to the Minister on certain matters, but in practice power lies with local education committees rather than with the Department of State.

The schools established by the Forster Act were 'all age'. This meant that a child (unless he were fortunate enough to win a free place * to the local grammar school at ten or eleven) spent all his school life in one building. There was no 'divide' between the stages of education – infant, junior, secondary – as there is today.

Broadly speaking, this was the position at the end of the First World War. Schools were administered at local authority level, but each authority received some financial support from central government. A proportion of the expenditure on education was levied from local rates and the monies so obtained were spent on both county and voluntary aided (Church) schools. County and Church schools co-existed, the only difference between the two often being the amount of direct sectarian teaching that was found in the Church schools.

The next big step forward – and the one most pertinent to our understanding of the contemporary English primary school – occurred in 1931 with the publication of the Hadow Report. This report, commissioned by the government, observed that 'Primary Education should be regarded as ending at about the

* In the academic year 1919–20, of 282,005 children enjoying secondary education, only 82,630 had free places and only six of 1,000 state-aided secondary schools did not charge fees.

age of 11 +. A second stage should then begin and this stage would end for many at 16 +, for some at 18 or 19 but for the majority at 14 + or 15 +.' Thus it was suggested, children of primary age were to be set apart from older 'secondary-stage' children; that new sorts of schools should be created – schools which met the needs of young children and schools which met the needs of the adolescent.

The 1930s saw a massive re-organization of education. Education now fell into two phases. Children attended an infant school until they were seven. This infant school was sometimes part of a junior school (which catered for seven to eleven year olds), sometimes it was quite independent. At eleven the child might transfer to a grammar or central (trade) school or remain in a 're-organized' secondary elementary school. By 1939 over two thirds of children of secondary age were attending re-organized schools. 'All-age' schools remained however, and even in 1949 36 per cent of children of secondary age were still attending schools which also housed children of primary school age.

The Second World War may have slowed down the changes begun by the Hadow Reports * but it did not prevent plans being made for education in the post-war years. In 1943 the Norwood Report made further recommendations – that secondary education should meet the needs of the three groups of pupils that made up the school population. These pupils should be taught in schools which met their particular needs – secondary grammar, secondary technical and secondary modern.

A year later the Butler Act was passed. Education was to be seen in three stages – primary, secondary and further. The importance of the first stage was implicit in the Act, but the problem of transfer remained. Grammar schools, rooted in tradition and offering courses to the age of eighteen, co-existed alongside the old elementary school. Even though these latter schools were given a new name (secondary modern) they were regarded by parents as the cinderellas of the educational world,

* There were three Hadow Reports: 1926 (adolescent children); 1931 (primary children); 1933 (nursery and infant children).

often offering a shorter course and having poorer facilities. Some local authorities (particularly in parts of the country where there was considerable post-war re-building) were able to build multilateral schools. These schools could be truly comprehensive, embracing under one roof children of all abilities and offering courses which were academic, technical and vocational. Unfortunately it was not possible to change secondary education overnight. In many areas the primary school was given the task of sorting children (at the age of eleven) to fit into the range of secondary schools that existed in its area. Often this selection was achieved by an examination, the results of which determined secondary placement, and this undoubtedly had a deadening effect upon the primary school curriculum. Further there was the danger that teachers (and parents) would come to regard the primary school simply as an academic hot house, an institution which was judged by the numbers of its pupils which were successful in a competitive examination at the age of eleven. The 'failures' (and nationwide these totalled 80 per cent of eleven year olds) were dispatched to secondary modern schools which, as a result, did not enjoy much of a reputation.

Since the mid-1950s secondary education has again been undergoing a gentle revolution. The realization that a test at eleven is not the most appropriate way to determine a child's future has led to the establishment of secondary schools to meet the needs of children of all academic abilities.

Comprehensive education (which is common to many countries across the world) has not come to England easily, for there is still the desire to preserve the traditions of schools which appear to have served the community so well in the past that to destroy them (in the interests of re-organization) seems to some to be an act of vandalism.

The Plowden Report, *Children and their Primary Schools*, was published in 1967 during this period of change. The primary school – its children and its teachers – had been freed from the shackles of the 11 +. The school could now concern itself with children's immediate needs. Academic excellence was not ignored, but academic ability was no longer the principal criterion for judging a child. The Plowden Report emphasized good practice and commented favourably upon a more enlightened approach to the education of the young child. As with all government reports, recommendations were made, of which one concerns us here.

It must be apparent that the age at which education commences within any institution (whether nursery school or university) is based upon an arbitrary decision. The Plowden Report questioned the length of time that children spent in infant schools and suggested that primary education should be reorganized into first schools and middle schools. In some areas this has happened, but like so much in English education there is no recognizable pattern, as the following table illustrates.

AREA A

    First schools (five to nine)
    Middle schools (nine to thirteen)
    Junior high (thirteen to sixteen plus)
    Senior high (sixteen plus and above)
    (Sixth-form college)

AREA B

    First schools (five to eight)
    Middle schools (eight to twelve)
    Secondary comprehensive (twelve upwards)

AREA C

    Infant schools (five to seven)
    Junior schools (seven to eleven)
    Secondary comprehensive (eleven to eighteen)
    and/or secondary grammar (eleven to eighteen)

AREA D

    Primary schools (five to eleven)
    Comprehensive schools (eleven to eighteen)

I have deliberately chosen to present these divisions in an abstract manner, unrelated to individual local authorities. However, it is worth noting that at the time of writing one metropolitan district of Yorkshire has within its area children changing schools at the age of five (from nursery to infant), seven (from infant to junior) and eight and nine (from first to middle), at eleven (from junior to secondary) and twelve and thirteen (from middle to high) and at sixteen (from secondary to sixth-form college. Obviously such diversity within one authority can create tremendous organization problems, both for the administrators, who have to make it work, and for parents, who have to cope with its variety.

To some readers the variety which is to be found in English schools may appear puzzling and confusing: to others it will suggest intellectual slackness, a lack of vision, a system devoid of purpose and direction. And yet, in my experience (based upon extended visits to many other countries), it is from diversity that the English school draws much of its own strength. Our schools – in their organization, the professional expectations of teacher and parent, their broad curriculum – continue to foster traditions rooted in the past. The children still assemble to say prayers; carol services and harvest festivals continue to mark the passing of the school year as they did in the 1880s and 1930s. But what diversity has brought is experiment in curriculum, in teaching styles, in school buildings. These experiments have resulted in a continual reappraisal of teaching and a better understanding of the way in which children learn.

Part Two   *The Curriculum*

5　*Language Arts*

The more I talk to parents about the education of the young child, the more I realize that for the great majority 'education' at primary level means the mastery of the written and spoken word.

The parent of the child who reads at six and a half feels 'he is getting on well at school,' even though his personal relationships may be appalling, his manners non-existent and his ability to cope in other subject areas quite minimal. At the same time, the parents of a seven year old whose reading is hesitant will like as not express all manner of anxieties about the future, for fluent mastery of the written word in late infancy is regarded as the key which will unlock the door to academic success in later life. The hesitant reader might have all the qualities necessary for a career in one of the learned professions – an ease of social relationship, a lively mind, the ability to concentrate, to sift material. But too often these remain unacknowledged in the headlong drive to master reading.

So where do the schools stand? Teachers cannot (nor should they) ignore parental expectations, and they cannot complacently wait until 'reading comes' (for the strain that this will impose upon the child would be unforgivable). At the same time, however, teachers cannot make a child read if he has not yet reached the stage of being able to interpret a page of symbols. The reasons for this inability might not be intellectual; emotional and physical disabilities are just as likely to slow down a child's progress as innate lack of intellectual capacity.

In the early stages of teaching reading (five to six plus), the child will be encouraged to look. To see a shape is not the same as to look at a shape, for to look closely at a shape means far more than just seeing it. Through careful looking children are helped to identify patterns, to become exact when numbers (represented by means of dots or objects) are involved. Games requiring matching (such as mosaics, jigsaws, dominoes) are played, pictures are discussed. All of this will help towards the development of a seeing eye, which will eventually be able to differentiate between the shape of 'here' and 'there' or 'in' and 'up' and 'it'.

Parallel with these 'looking' activities the children will be handling books. Initially these books may have no words, but contain pictures which by themselves tell a simple story. The role that picture books play in the teaching of reading should not be underestimated, for not only do they teach children how to handle books but they also encourage the use and development of speech. Writing (and the decoding of it through reading) is nothing more than a way of recording words; speech (the words people use) may be written, and, having been written down, may be read and thus spoken. The interrelationship of words in all their forms lies at the centre of all the young child's activities in school. Words are presented as constant things – the child speaks his news, tells his story, draws his picture. He is then helped to write the words he needs to record his story or to explain his picture. These early efforts may only be writing over a sentence prepared by the teacher or, as manual control improves, copying out a sentence beneath the teacher's script. Slowly, however, certain words will be mastered, words which the child can identify visually (Here is . . . , There is . . .), speak (read aloud) and record. The constancy of words, that they are unchanging in format and meaning and are found everywhere (on television, on advertisement hoardings, in newspapers, on boxes, in books), is probably too obvious a point for me to labour here, but it is a point continually stressed by teachers in the early stages of language teaching.

The basic primers that most schools use underpin and provide a structure for this work. But although they serve to introduce children to reading through a basic vocabulary, they are rarely regarded as anything more than an aid. In other words, because Peter or Mary have not read to a teacher on a particular day from their primer it does not mean that their reading skills are being ignored.

There is a growing tendency to make more than one reading scheme (that is, commercially produced primers) available, although this is not always the case in those schools which are following a very specific reading programme. Some schemes for instance build in a colour element with different colour combinations providing 'clues' to help interpret the written symbols. If the Initial Teaching Alphabet (developed by Pitman as a means of introducing children to reading through a specially devised and extended alphabet) is being used, all work is usually presented in it (class notices, names, stories), which will tend to reduce the range of material available. Reading schemes based on colour or an extended alphabet are attempts to help children to overcome the complex structure of written English and readily identify its more difficult phonic characteristics. Incidentally there is no evidence that the use of ITA in any way hampers children when they move at about seven, to traditional script although it is much less widely used today than it was when it was first introduced in the early 1960s.

'Breakthrough to Literacy' is an approach to language teaching which is to be found in an increasing number of schools. 'Breakthrough' was developed by a team of teachers in an attempt to unite all aspects of language development. Each child has a 'sentence maker', a board which holds the words he wishes to use. These words can be arranged in any order so that sentences, simple and complex, can be built up as required. 'Breakthrough' is based upon the belief that reading is most successfully mastered when the words a child uses in his everyday life are incorporated into his reading programme. To some extent its very success and popularity are a condemnation of some of the more traditional schemes whose language is quite foreign to that normally used by children. The sentence 'Come, John, come see the ducks' introduces both consonants and vowels but continual repetition of such construction is hardly likely to fire a diffident reader with enthusiasm and encourage him to struggle on through pages which tell of 'John going up, up, up while Mary goes down, down, down'.

Reading, in the first two years of school, should be regarded, then, as part of a language programme, not as an activity divorced from everything else that goes on in the classroom. Because young children learn by asking questions, by experimenting with words spoken and written, by talking, a classroom full of children of infant age is rarely a rigidly ordered, silent place. Indeed it is appropriate that it should not be so. Most infant schools contain a few children whose homes are so verbally rich that the classroom merely acts as a place where language can be used; but for the majority of children the new experiences of school result in the development of an ever-widening vocabulary, and this vocabulary has to be continually used in order to be adequately mastered. The 'busy' working sound of a typical infant classroom should not be interpreted as an indication of wayward teaching. Language spoken is the foundation of language written.

Language and the feel for words that good teaching inspires also come from listening to stories well read. Throughout the primary years children listen avidly to imaginative verse, to ballads, to descriptive prose, to autobiography, to fiction of all kinds. Periods of rapt listening must be set against periods of involved discussion, for a good school will provide opportunity for both. A well-presented story read aloud does much to inspire children with a love of books, for through the written word a young child is able to gain entry to that rich world of fantasy and adventure which plays such an important part in intellectual and emotional development in the years preceding adolescence.

Although reading is seen as one of a number of language activities, its mastery at a reasonably early stage in the education process is vital if the child is to make maximum use of the facilities available. To learn to read a child needs practice – the actual reading of passages to an adult (or to another child who can read well). Many schools 'employ' parents (on a voluntary basis) to listen to individual children and most parents 'hear' their children read at home. Success is quickened by regular reading aloud, provided, of course, that the listener is sympathetic to the difficulties that the reader experiences. The importance of reading for pleasure (as contrasted to reading as a technical skill) is stressed by most schools, which is why there is still a suspicion in the minds of some teachers that enthusiastic parents may unwittingly undermine confidence by placing undue concentration upon those words that a child has not yet learned rather than expressing delight in those that he has.

The technical rules of reading (and thus, indirectly, spelling) continue to be taught throughout the child's primary school life. Phonics are taught in the early years, beginning with the basic sounds that individual letters make and extending this to include such things as diphthongs and word endings. In the majority of schools the phonic approach is not the only method used. Children also learn to read by learning the shapes that individual words make. This helps explain why a child who confuses 'where' and 'when' can often recognize the words 'elephant' or 'telephone'. Flash cards, word lists, dictionaries, work books all tend to reflect this mixture of approach. Indeed it is not uncommon for a child who has failed quite miserably with one approach to reading to be introduced to another scheme where the emphasis is entirely different – and for the second scheme to succeed.

It is salutary to note that despite all the knowledge we have about children, their aptitudes and their needs, there is still no clear insight into how they learn to read, or how we can determine the point in their development which marks the transition from non reader to reader. Teachers use the term 'reading readiness' to describe that point when a child seems to be on the brink of reading, but the great divide between 'reading readiness' and 'reading sufficiency' is one which has not yet been extensively analysed. For some children the transition from readiness to self-sufficiency takes a few months, for others it will take several painstaking and plodding years. I have known children who have moved from reading primers to the *Sunday Times* in a matter of months and others who enter the secondary stage of their education with a reading level that is little more than rudimentary.

Reading by itself does not constitute literacy. To read successfully one also has to read with understanding. Most children, as soon as they have mastered the basic rules of reading, will be given work connected with the passages they have read. This work might be based on cards made by the teacher or on books of comprehension exercises, exercises which are often as dull and uninspired as they were when I went to school thirty years ago. Modern four-colour printing might have updated the image, but the purpose of the exercises (to show the meaning of words, to manipulate tenses, to précis paragraphs and to re-phrase perfectly good English) remains unchanged. In schools where the completion of pages of exercises is a less obvious curriculum objective, understanding will be tested in a variety of ways, for example by direct oral questioning and discussion, or by observing individual children's response to the spoken word and to written instructions (for example in science experi-ments and in following plans in constructional kits).

Understanding can also be formally tested. A number of standardized tests are now in use which give a reliable indica-tion of a child's ability to read as well as his understanding of what he has read.

Most primary schools at some stage test the children's read-ing ability. A variety of tests are used, but most modern tests show a high degree of correlation one with another. Children are rarely tested at the infant stage; the crisis point, as the Bullock Report on Literacy (1975) stressed, comes after seven, when, if a child is not beginning to read independently, he begins to be at a considerable disadvantage in all areas of his school life, social as well as academic.

The material used to test children has been extensively re-searched. A reading test may consist of lists of words or simple sentences or groups of words which the child has first to read aloud and then respond to, such as 'Is a red ball black?' The point at which the child can no longer continue (because his reading is inadequate) indicates his reading age. This age (which is usually given in years and months) represents the point in the test which will be reached by the average child of that age. Thus if an eight and a half year old achieves a reading age of eight years six months the score would suggest that he is functioning at an acceptable level for his age group. A score of six years three months, however, would indicate that he is at least two years behind that which might be expected of a child of his age group (an alternative way of regarding the score is that he is reading at the level of a six and a quarter year old). If our imaginary child obtained a score of twelve years, he would be a fluent reader with a reading score some three years in advance of his age.

These results are not always expressed as reading ages (that is, in years and months). Sometimes the term 'reading quotient' is used. This is obtained by using the formula

$$\frac{\text{Reading age}}{\text{Chronological age}} \times 100$$

Applying the scores given in the examples above, the following quotients are obtained.

				Quotient
Score A	Score	8 yrs 6 m	$= \dfrac{8 \cdot 5}{8 \cdot 5} \times 100$	100
	Age	8 yrs 6 m		
Score B	Score	6 yrs 3 m	$= \dfrac{6 \cdot 25}{8 \cdot 5} \times 100$	73·5
	Age	8 yrs 6 m		
Score C	Score	12 yrs	$= \dfrac{12 \cdot 0}{8 \cdot 5} \times 100$	141·2
	Age	8 yrs 6 m		

Taking 100 as the base which represents the performance of the average child, example B shows a score 26½ points below this and example C a score of 41 points above it.

Reading ages and reading quotients are useful indications of a child's progress in relation to his peer group. But, as in all tests, the scores can be taken too seriously. There has been much public discussion in recent years on the subject of reading standards, a discussion based not so much on proved statistics but on an uneasy feeling that eleven year olds were not reading as fluently as preceding generations had done. The Bullock Report did not confirm these feelings. It did, however, make the point that whereas standards had not actually gone down they had not gone up either.

It would be foolish to expect that ever-increasing expenditure on educational provision will result in a steady increase of standards in all subject areas. But schools have a responsibility to see that children are given the opportunity to develop their language skills to the full, and a complacent attitude – 'things are not much better, but they are no worse' – is quite unacceptable. The Bullock Report has affected schools. It served to spotlight the place of language in the curriculum and in giving opportunity for public concern to be expressed it forced schools to re-examine their programmes. It is significant that in the period following its publication such statistics as have been released suggest that reading standards for eleven year olds are beginning to rise once more.

As reading progresses, so will writing; the two activities have so much in common that success in one invariably has some effect upon the other.

Before describing the range of writing which may be found in primary schools it would be appropriate to consider briefly the problems which children face when first attempting to record their thoughts on paper. I have worked with many young children who at the age of six are fluent readers but who find it extremely difficult to write. Often these children are academically above average – some of them could be described as 'high fliers' – yet the physical difficulties they experience in controlling the marks made by their pencil have to be seen to be believed. In these early years this frustration needs to be appreciated by all the adults in the child's life. In school, manual dexterity will be developed through picture-making, using a wide variety of media, as well as through the ordered and systematic teaching of handwriting. Meanwhile parents need to be aware that the ability of the brain to translate printed symbols should not be taken to mean that the same brain is good at controlling pencils, crayons or felt-tipped pens. To support children who have poor manual dexterity, some schools have encouraged children to use typewriters for a proportion of their written work.

For many children the early years of childhood are rich in words. Through words a child arrives at an understanding of his world, for words not only have concrete meaning but also express emotion. By using words a child learns to communicate and reach out to other people, first to members of his own family and then to the community beyond. Words provide a pathway to knowledge, a means of clarifying discoveries, an outlet for fears, anxieties and tensions. By manipulating words in particular ways patterns of speech evolve, patterns which remain to bedevil our adult life, to identify our birthplace, the community into which we were born. From simple one-word and two-word sentences, the structures proliferate and become complex. The four year old who asks whether 'the angels wear soft shoes because otherwise it would be noisy in heaven with all those people moving around' is using words to express thoughts. But if the thoughts are complex, so are the word structures that she uses for expressing them.

This four year old might well find herself, at five, in a class which contains some children who have never been encouraged to talk, to think their thoughts in words, children who have never been given words to think with. Coping with linguistic poverty as well as linguistic richness is part of the primary teacher's task. The talking which characterizes much of school life today is often contrasted with the long silences which were an accepted part of school ritual of forty years ago. However, for the majority of teachers the development of writing goes hand in hand with the extension of the spoken word.

This means that the successful teacher will largely draw upon the child's experiences when providing opportunities for talking and such writing as may follow upon it. The daily diary or newsbook which remains a feature of many infant schools depends for its success upon how well personal experiences can be drawn out of the child. The six year old in a school I was visiting who observed (as she struggled over a diary entry) 'No news ever happens to me' highlights the danger of the thoughtless, ill-prepared diary. 'No one here,' she was saying, 'has helped me see something worth writing about in my daily life.'

Throughout the primary years the teacher is helping children to draw upon their own experiences and to give them the opportunity to express their own viewpoints and visions. Words, after all, have to be interpreted in the light of individual experience. This is not to say that we should never expect children to write about intangible things or about things they can never have experienced, but rather that we should not judge them too harshly when their work is less accomplished than usual as a result of being asked to do so.

The link that written English has with all the other areas of the curriculum does allow, of course, for real experiences to be written about. The exploration of a stream, the visit to the smith to watch a horse being shod, the description of a room in a castle, the observation of classroom pets, the recording of a science experiment, all provide opportunity for writing.

'I went to see the horses shod. I was standing next to John. There was this wasp. It kept flying round him and it kept making him move and Mrs Johns got cross and said stand still. The smith sort of bent the shoes until they were hot. They sizzled when he put them in the water. John didn't get stung. The smith's name was Joe.' This is a typically personal account of a happening, written by a seven year old, full of the events which made the visit significant *for him*.

Such writing is common in the first four years of schooling, for here the writing interweaves thoughts and feelings as well as facts.

'My Mum had a baby at home, it was a boy called William and we needed ever such a lot of hot water for the nurse, my Dad said he'd never be able to afford the gas bill.'

This example from a six year old contains these elements. It also illustrates a further quality of early writing. The reader has somehow to imagine a child speaking and build in his own pauses.

The years from seven to eleven see children moving from this intensely free-flowing style to one which, though still personal, begins to be disciplined by the conventions of the language. Punctuation (which is no more than good manners in writing) is introduced (though sparingly), spellings are corrected and basic sentence construction leading into paragraphing will be touched upon. The dilemmas facing the teacher here are many. Should I encourage free-flowing writing or do I check their flow by insisting on careful punctuation? Do I praise a child for choosing the word 'deeliberat' to describe an action or observe that 'careful' would do almost as well and it's easier to spell? Do I encourage only correct usage of words and phrases, or do I praise the child who is outrageous in his use of words but by being so achieves a high level of drama in his final presentation? In an attempt to solve these difficulties some teachers retreat into textbooks with pages of exercises which, if slavishly followed, will result (it is hoped) in the correct use of speech marks, an understanding of the semi-colon and the significance of the adjectival phrase. This analysis of the written word is far less common than it was in the past, and few teachers would now argue that such exercises occupy a central place in the language development of the young child. They did serve to keep children quiet, however, which is why they are remembered by generations of parents and why their absence today serves to confirm the impression that education is not what it was!

The pattern of the words we use, the shape that our sentences follow are not arrived at by working pages of exercises. The whole climate of the modern primary school is aimed at helping children to use words to express their vision and viewpoint unambiguously. 'Creative writing' is not seen as an alternative to factual reporting but as an activity which complements it. Creative writing is perhaps an unfortunate term, for the media have used it almost as a term of abuse, identifying it with the worst excesses of modern methods, such as poor spelling, indifferent punctuation and ill-constructed sentences. Anyone who has written, however, will appreciate that to produce any writing of quality, whether factual or free and imaginative, has to search for words, to refine words and phrases, to ensure that meaning is accurately conveyed. Children who are being taught to write, whether creatively or on factual topics, will often need to be given the opportunity to re-shape their written thoughts before presenting them in their final form. It is for this reason that 'work books' in which children write – on demand – descriptions of their cat or of washing day, or a poem entitled 'highway adventure', are becoming less and less common. The idea is presented, it is talked about, written work is begun and corrected until a balanced piece of writing, acceptable to both teacher and child, is achieved. This is not weak teaching. It is quite the reverse. Words do not simply flow on demand, as a cursory glance at the original manuscripts of writers of genius would quickly confirm. As adults we ought to remember the number of attempts we sometimes make before arriving at the most appropriate style when writing a letter to a bank manager, a headteacher or to the servicing manager of the local garage. For some reason what we, mature adults, cannot do with words (create instant statements) we expect our children to do almost effortlessly.

Paradoxically, as teachers were discovering that, given time, many children could write in a style which incorporates personal vision as well as structure and order, the very freedoms within schools which have allowed them to do so have been criticized so stridently. The following examples of children's writing illustrate something of the qualities which I would be loath to see disappear from the primary classroom.

On teeth

These writings followed some discussion on teeth and a visit by a dentist to school to talk about oral hygiene.

My Grandpa, he's a dentist, but he's got false teeth. (*five year old*)

The dentist squirted some air on my teeth. I closed my mouth by mistake and bit him. He said 'Ow'. (*six year old*)

The dentist gets hard fingers because people bite them. (*six year old*)

If I keep eating sweets my teeth will fall out. But I like sweets. (*six year old*)

When it was my turn I went in and it smelt clean and it smelt of fluoride. The dentist drilled a hole in my tooth and put a piece of cotton wool in my mouth to keep it dry. If he didn't all the germs would collect in the hole. (*seven year old*)

The dentist told us the funniest thing. When he first gave an injection the liquid went down the man's throat and he couldn't feel himself breathing and he tried to get away. He struggled so much he split his trousers. (*seven year old*)

On holiday

> I went to Weston House
> I saw a rabbit
> I saw lots of baby ducks
> The peacocks had big tails
> I saw a potter and played
> on a climbing frame.
> > (*five year old*)

I went to Norfolk. I saw an old castle. Long ago it looked like this (picture). Now it is ruin. I photographed an arch. I went to Oxburgh Hall. It had beautiful furniture and twisted chimney pots. (*six year old*)

After visiting Bristol

Isambard Kingdom Brunel built the S.S. Great Britain in 1843. The S.S. Great Britain was the first ever iron ship to sail the Atlantic Ocean. When they first tried the ship out they used animals as passengers because people said it would sink. On the boat's fifth voyage a fog came down and it landed on the coast of Ireland. It took sixty days to mend. (*seven year old*)

At Ryedale

We saw a very old cruck house. A cruck house is made with oak beams like this. Two beams are put upwards making an arch. Then a long pole is put on the top and two other poles are put on each side. There can be as many arches as you like. On top of the three poles there are rafters, on top of the rafters, thatch. One side of the cruck house is for the people, the other side is for the animals. The cruck house I saw has a salt box in the fireplace. Salt was precious so the King put a tax on it and to keep the salt dry people would put a salt box near the fire. The person sitting nearest the salt is the most important person. The cruck house had a witch post to keep evil spirits away. (*eight year old*)

Boscobel House

Boscobel House was an old house where Charles II had hidden when he was being hunted by Cromwell and his soldiers. There was a priest hole. It was a very tiny room five feet long and five feet wide. Charles, who was 6 ft 2 ins tall, couldn't have stood up in it. Boscobel House used to be in a forest, but there are only a few trees growing now. One of the trees is descended from the tree Charles hid in. It now has a metal fence round it. In Boscobel House is a secret doorway so you can get out into the forest if you were in a rush. (*eight year old*)

The lighthouse

We went to the lighthouse. The keeper talked about the engine. Then we went upstairs and saw where the emergency light was housed. We went up some much steeper steps to the big light. It was made up of little prisms. There was a spare light on the side so if the other went off the spare one came on. The light flashed three times every twenty seconds. The light was of 10,000 candle power. The light would cost £30,000 to replace. (*nine year old*)

Anemones

We went on the beach. I found a Beadlet anemone. The Beadlet anemone can be red, brown or green. The one we found was red and had no pattern on its discs and tentacles. The Beadlet gets its name from the blue dots inside the rim.

The tentacles are used to get food. On the tentacles are poisonous darts which shoot out and stun the prey. Then the tentacles bring the prey into the mouth at the centre.

The sea anemone moves along on a big foot that sticks to the rocks. When you take an anemone from the water it looks horrible, but when you put it back it looks beautiful. (*ten year old*)

The paste factory at Chichester

We set off for the paste factory. A lady met us and took us round. First we saw the chickens being cooked, then people pulling chickens apart, then the rest of the chicken being mashed up. We saw lots of jars being sterilized and filled with chicken paste. In one room there was a balcony and we could look down on the machines. Some machines were filling pots, some were putting labels on pots and some were putting the pots into packs and covering these with polythene. The whole place smelt horrid. The lady told us that there were two million pots in that room.

When we had gone round I thought, 'I'll never go near meat paste again.'

To make me feel worse, at the end, she gave me a free pot to take home. (*eleven year old*)

Wind and sand

The wind is blowing the sand into my eyes
It seems like a sand storm
The sand is whirling round and round
It envelopes me

Pebbles are shining until the wind blows
They are covered with sand
I hate the beach on a windy day
The sand gets into my eyes
I cannot see.

(*seven year old*)

Mill Mouse

I live in the mill and feed off the grain
It's quite good food, though a little plain
The miller has a cat, we're careful of him
For if he caught us, he'd tear every limb
The cat is my enemy
The rat is my friend
I am simply a mill mouse
And that is the end.

(*eight year old*)

Spider

There is a spider in my bath
Her legs are long
She cowers in a corner
Shall I kill her?
But I think
'She has life as well as me
To kill her would be to take a life.'

But I hate the spider
Her legs are hairy
I am frightened as she crawls towards me
What are looks to feelings?
She may be kind and happy
She may be cruel and evil
Shall I kill her?

Then, before I can think anymore
She disappears down the plughole
I am left thinking
Should I have killed her?
If it's not a crime to kill a spider
Why is it a crime to kill a man?

(*nine year old*)

Prisons

I am in prison in the world.
I am in prison in my family.
I am in prison in my mind.
Everybody is in prison in some way.
But think about the real prisoners,
Think about people who are in those
Dark and dreary buildings
With nothing to do but sit and sleep,
Or think about the outside world
Of their wives or husbands or children.
As the years go by they lose all their hope
Until they haven't got a wish in the world.
Finally they lose their senses
And care about nothing.

(*nine year old*)

An old man

Look at him
An old, bedraggled figure standing there in the rain.
He's on the threshold of the house of death
Stepping forward on the ever thinning ice of time
Dying, like a flower picked from the sweet grass.
Once he was youthful
And now look!
He used to be energetic,
Running, fighting.

Even when he was married he was young
Compared to now.
He was young!
He is like a tree rid of leaves, blossoms and fruit.
He's between life and death.
For him soon the sun will go down forever.
Let him keep his idea of hope to himself.
Let him be confident and fall into the hands of death unhurt.
Let him die peacefully when all his hopes are gone.
His frozen tears sparkle in the evening light.

(ten year old)

An old lady

She was now 100
100 years I'm sure
She'd struggled round old London town
And couldn't struggle more.
If she'd been born in a house
With window panes of glass
She wouldn't have had this horrid idea
And this wouldn't have come to pass.
'I'm tired of living,' she said
'I'm tired of living,' said she
'I sleep on a bed of newspapers
For I cannot pay a fee.'
She went down to the river Thames,
This was all she could do.
She stood by the deep dark water
But couldn't do it, she knew.
She hadn't had a bad life,
Even though she was so poor.
She'd spent her money on good old drink,
But there wasn't any more.
'I'm tired of living,' she said,
'But I don't want to leave right now,
I must, I must, I'm going to,

I'm going to do it, but how?'
She looked at the deep dark water
And remembered what she'd said
'I am tired of living,'
There was just one tear she shed.
From one of her inner pockets
A little knife she brought,
She screamed, 'I go at my own free will,'
Her death was brief and short.
She lay in the rippling water,
Her worries had flowed away,
Her clothes were floating round her,
She had nothing more to say.
Nobody saw the body,
Nobody seemed to care,
It didn't matter to anyone
That she was lying there.

(eleven year old)

These examples serve to illustrate the challenges involved in writing. As adults we may be expected to write the occasional letter to family and friends, or (less rarely) to make notes on a project at work. But whereas most adults write rarely, children are expected to convey ideas in writing on almost every day of their life in school. The topics that they are asked to write about are not necessarily related to their interests, for often (even in schools sympathetic to children's needs) they are invited to write about things in which they have no interest whatsoever.

Writings of the kind included here come when teacher and taught are able to accept the discipline and demands of writing. If the setting down of words on paper requires thought, care and sensitivity, it requires an equal measure of these qualities to mark them as a teacher or to evaluate them as a critic. In classrooms (whether formal or informal) where trust and understanding are absent, there will be little writing of quality.

It has been said that every activity a child undertakes in

school is also a lesson in English, for without communication there can be little learning. Throughout their school day opportunity is given to children to express themselves through words spoken and written. It is to these other areas, where language provides the vehicle for learning, that we will turn our attention in the chapters that follow.

6 Number

Of all the changes that have taken place in primary education since the end of the war, none has been more profound or far-reaching than those in the field of mathematics. Instead of working pages of mechanical sums, children are learning something of the language of sets, instead of chanting tables they are exploring such things as symmetry and reflection.

There are a number of reasons for this shift of emphasis. Perhaps the most obvious reason for change lay in the fact that traditional methods had not been very successful. The bulk of the adult population seemed to have little understanding of mathematics, and the majority of the secondary school leavers who were joining the work force in the early 1950s showed no more aptitude for the subject than their parents had done. The social and economic climate of the period did little to dispel this feeling of disenchantment with mathematics. We were moving into a world of computers, electric adding machines were appearing in the new supermarkets; the army of ledger clerks who had serviced Britain's industry at the turn of the century were no longer required.

These influences were reflected in the schools and universities. No longer was mathematics required for university entrance. Unlike its predecessor * the General Certificate of Education could be obtained without mathematics. Indeed even respected educationalists observed quite publicly that mathematics had been 'somewhat over-emphasized'. After all (the argument went on) what mathematics does the average person

---

*To obtain a School Certificate (which GCE replaced) the candidate was required to obtain passes in at least six subjects. To obtain this certificate at matriculation level (a recognized university entrance requirement) the candidate needed to obtain credits in five subjects, one of which had to be mathematics. The examination was usually taken at the age of sixteen.

use in the everyday business of living – some counting, an ability to reckon money and cope with his personal accounts, tell the time, read a calendar, use a simple measure. And to some extent such observations contained more than a grain of truth. Teachers in primary schools (to say nothing of their colleagues at secondary level) had little to show for their labours. The work force might not be illiterate, but it could hardly be described as numerate.

The regime followed by many primary schools in the early 1950's did little to change this rather bleak situation. Selection at eleven (for grammar school placement) was common to all local education authorities and the papers which were set in mathematics were designed to identify those children who could manipulate numbers quickly. A mastery of arithmetical tricks was essential to success, and as a result, the mathematical content of the curriculum tended to be meagre. But if it was mean and meagre for the bright child it was largely meaningless for the 80 to 90 per cent of the pupils who would fail the selection process. Failure was built into the education process – irrelevances were taught to the many for the supposed benefit of the few.

Fortunately, other more positive influences were making themselves felt. In *Primary Education* (HMSO, 1952) inspectors from the Ministry of Education, as it then was, argued that mathematics should occupy a central place in the curriculum, for it is 'a continuing and unique way of thought and children should be acquainted with it and experience it'. While this quietly persuasive voice aimed at focusing attention on the cultural contribution that a study of mathematics could make in the education of young people, teachers and administrators were making their own more dramatic efforts to sweep away the rigid, outmoded techniques of traditional classroom practice.

However, it would be wrong to think that this was a national, tightly organized movement. It drew its strength from teachers working in small groups, discussing and planning the mathematical content of the primary school curriculum relating their findings to the children with whom they worked and discovering with them something of the fascination that numbers, patterns and shapes hold for us all. These discussion groups were supported by teachers for whom mathematics was their academic discipline (as tutors in universities and polytechnics), by secondary school teachers who were dealing, day by day, with children who had learned to hate mathematics and by primary and nursery school teachers who had a vital part to play if children were to have the right sort of mathematical experiences in their early days in school.

In England much credit must go to Edith Biggs, an indefatigable enthusiast, who was employed as a staff inspector at the Department of Education and Science. With her lectures and practical workshops Edith Biggs co-ordinated the work of different groups and focused attention upon the poverty of mathematics teaching in our schools, drawing teachers' attention to the relevance of the work of a Swiss psychologist – Jean Piaget.

Piaget argued that in the past the majority of children were introduced to formal number teaching long before they were ready to learn with understanding. Too much emphasis had been placed upon mechanical learning and not enough upon relational thinking. Learning based on class instruction and the passive absorption of facts might lead to a small number of children who were proficient in calculation. But its by product was a large number of children who could only be described as mathematically inept.

Briefly – for it does not fall within my brief to analyse Piaget's work even if I were competent to do so – Piaget suggests that children pass through three distinct developmental stages in their mastery of mathematics. In the pre-operational stage the child has little idea of number and is quite unable to deal with the simplest of number situations with understanding. He is deceived by what he sees. Thus, to give an example from my own recent experience, a doctor treating a five year old child in hospital required a blood sample. When taken, John protested that soon 'he would have no blood left'. The doctor reassured him, saying, 'Look, I've only taken a little,' and held up the long thin pipette in which the blood was stored. At this John was even more inconsolable; 'But that's a bigger bottle than the one Mummy gets from the milkman.' John had not grasped that the height of the two bottles was only one of the elements which had to be taken into account when attempting to determine the volume of blood that each would hold. He was deceived by what he saw.

Although Piaget does not label this stage as being appropriate to a particular age group, many children when they enter school are at this basic level of reasoning. Just as teachers use the term 'reading-readiness' to describe activities a child undertakes before he learns to read, in mathematics the term 'number readiness' could be used to describe the activities which are introduced before the next stage in conceptual development is reached.

The intuitive stage follows. At this stage children are able to grasp basic relationships provided the numbers involved are small. Thus while adults can accept that $4+6$ is the same as $6+4$ (for example) young children are much less trusting of the nature of numbers. Yet, and herein lies the principal difficulty for parent and teacher, an understanding of such truths is fundamental to any subsequent mathematical development. There is no denying that some children can, as a result of rote learning, master a number of arithmetical tricks (like carrying ten *) in the first year of schooling.

The value of Piaget's work is that it questions the wisdom of much of the content of the traditional curriculum and suggests other more useful and relevant ways of developing mathematical concepts.

The operational stage develops from the intuitive stage. At this level the child has firmly grasped the nature of number. To be able to describe ten, for example, in the following ways re-

---

*The thoughtful reader would do well to pause here to examine the term 'carrying ten'. In everyday life 'carry' has quite a different meaning from that given it in this context. And how many children, I wonder, have any understanding of the ten they carry, where they get it from and why they 'carry' it to another column only to leave it there!

quires considerable understanding of the principle underlying mathematical processes:

10 is made up of 5 groups of 2	(5×2)
10 is made up of 5 and 5 more	$(5 + 5)$
10 is made up of 2 groups of 5	(2×5)
10 is made up of 1 group of 4 and another group of 6	$(4 + 6)$
10 is made up of 1 group of 6 and another group of 4	$(6 + 4)$
10 is made up of 2 groups of 4 and 1 group of 2	$(2 \times 4) + (1 \times 2)$

In this example, which for simplicity I have taken from basic arithmetical computation, the child has moved towards a real appreciation of the meaning of ten. 'Ten', of itself, is meaningless. Ten what? Ten is a conceptualization, an abstract, an idea. In the contemporary primary school the aim is to give children an appreciation of numbers, the relationships which bind one to another, the patterns that they make. It is important that these fundamentals are grasped before children are asked (as I was at school) to borrow ten, pay back ten, bring down ten and do lots of other things to ten which are impossible (without considerable understanding of the nature of number) to justify.

Perhaps the most appropriate way of appreciating the changes in teaching method is to consider how as a young teacher I was expected to teach subtraction. To solve $170 - 89$ the following strategy was followed:

170   Begin with the unit column 0—9, we cannot.
89—   Borrow ten.

The sum now reads
$$\begin{array}{r} 1 \\ 170 \\ \underline{89-} \end{array}$$

Having 'borrowed' ten, it has to be paid back. Thus we arrive at
$$\begin{array}{r} 1 \\ 170 \\ \underline{9} \\ 89- \\ \hline \end{array}$$
(Pause for a moment. Why did the 8 become 9, and why did we borrow from the bottom line which we are subtracting from the top line? Why is the ten only shown as a figure 1?)

However we are not concerned with understanding, only with doing, so the process continues.

$$\begin{array}{r} \overset{1}{170} \\ {}^{9} \\ \underline{89-} \\ 1 \end{array}$$ 10 take away 9 leaves 1. Put one in the answer box and move to the next column.

Now we have reached the second stage of the sum, only to find that the process (described above) has to be repeated. 7—9 we cannot. Borrow 10. Pay it back to the bottom line. But there isn't a number below (the column is empty), so we take one and put in the figure 1 to show that we have.

The sum now looks like this. $$\begin{array}{r} \overset{1}{170} \\ {}^{9} \\ \underline{89} \\ 1 \end{array}$$

At this point ten must have taken on incredible properties in the minds of some children. I expect some did ask themselves whether there was a different sort of ten in the second column and wonder how a sum which began as 170—89 ended up looking like 170—199. But let the technique grind on to the end.

17—9   leaves 8
1—1   leaves 0

to leave the sum appearing thus* $$\begin{array}{r} \overset{1\,1}{170} \\ {}^{9} \\ \underline{89-} \\ 81 \end{array}$$

Some schools still use the 'carrying ten' method, some 'count on' (like the shop assistant), while others prefer to 'decompose

* In contrast shop assistants invariably 'counted on' when giving change. For example, having spent 13s. 9d. from £1 the conversation, as the change was counted out, ran like this, '13s. 9d. and 3d. is fourteen shillings and six more make a pound'. The sum 170—89 could have been solved in an identical manner (89 to 100 is 11. 11+70=81), but then – as now – many teachers fight shy of relating the realities of the world outside to classroom practice!

the ten', a method which, though somewhat long-winded, has the advantage of logicality. This method is as follows:

170   Begin with the unit column 0—9 we cannot.
89—

Break down the 7 tens in the next column into 6 tens and 1 ten. This 1 ten we decompose into units.

The sum now reads

$$\begin{array}{r} {}^{6}\ {}^{10+} \\ 1\ \ 7\ \ 0 \\ 8\ \ 9- \end{array}$$

Turning again to the units we now have $(10+0)-9=1$.

The sum now reads

$$\begin{array}{r} {}^{6}\ {}^{10+} \\ 1\ \ 7\ \ 0 \\ \underline{8\ \ 9-} \\ 1 \end{array}$$

We use the same technique for $6-8$.
6 (tens) -8 (tens) we cannot.
Break down the hundreds into 'lots of ten'.

This gives us

$$\begin{array}{r} {}^{0}\ {}^{10+6}\ {}^{10+} \\ 1\ \ 7\ \ 0 \\ \underline{8\ \ 9-} \\ 1 \end{array}$$

We can now work the tens column $(10+6)-8=8$. The hundred's column, being empty, the sum is completed.

$$\begin{array}{r} {}^{0}\ {}^{10+6}\ {}^{10+} \\ 1\ \ 7\ \ 0 \\ \underline{8\ \ 9-} \\ (0)\ \ 8\ \ 1 \end{array}$$

Most schools today use both 'counting on' and decomposition to teach subtraction. By teaching both methods children learn something of the ways numbers behave and techniques of problem-solving.

When tortuous teaching of the sort detailed in my first example is questioned (for such methods still have their supporters today) critics of the modern approaches to the teaching of mathematics have suggested, by way of justification, that the rote learning enabled children to 'do' pages of sums. In my experience, however, tricks taught without understanding are of little value. Children master them for the moment, only to forget them when new processes are introduced. Generations of teachers would testify to the fact that children who can cope with sums involving one type of operation (such as multiplication) can quickly become very confused when presented with a page of sums which involve a variety of operations. It is as though they have been taught processes which they are unable to relate to specific problems. They know, but they do not understand. As mathematics is a study of relationships, it is unlikely that much future progress will be made if the initial processes are ill-learned, ill-presented and poorly grasped.

The influence of Piaget has been profound. His findings indicated how little we understand of children's thinking and how much we had taken for granted. Reappraisal of the content of the curriculum and a review of teaching methods in an area as important as mathematics has provoked considerable discussion, and Piaget's research has not gone entirely unquestioned. His work specifically related to children living in Geneva. Did such research apply to children living in other cities, in other countries? Recent research has suggested that the stages of development which Piaget describes are accurate, but that each stage is reached rather earlier than Piaget's findings would suggest. Discussion in professional circles, therefore, has not centred upon the fundamentals of his research but rather upon the point in a child's development to which they apply.

Piaget argued that the three stages he defined (pre-operational, intuitive, operational), could be applied to all areas of mathematics. It was inappropriate to teach place value (for example) by setting pages of tens and units sums when a child was at the pre-operational stage of development. Not only was it irrelevant to teach a number process before children were intellectually ready to receive it, but such teaching was a waste of time and effort and could do irreparable harm to a child's future understanding of number. Thus, whether the aim of the teacher was to introduce the concept of conservation of number, series and pattern, equivalence, the difference between ordinal and cardinal numbers, a child's ability to cope with these abstract ideas would depend upon his level of mathematical thinking.

It is in this area that Piaget's research has led to considerable misunderstanding. I have met many parents who assume that because their seven year old is not producing page upon page of recognizable sums he is not learning mathematics. It is not easy to persuade a parent for whom the mastery of largely meaningless number drills were the central part of each school day that their child's teacher is concerned with the development of logical thinking, that understanding that $4+5$ implies $5+4$, $9-5$ and $9-4$ is of far greater importance than forty subtraction sums neatly presented.

The language of mathematics has added yet another difficulty. In the past the language of number was largely ignored, and as a consequence teachers now find it difficult to explain to parents the intricacies of the programme they are following in school. This confusion is further deepened by their children who come home from school and talk of sets, topology and ordered pairs.

To this breakdown of dialogue is added one further dimension. Such mathematical discoveries as are recorded by young children do not follow the traditional forms. Mathematics is a precise science and such recordings as children do make should be precise and orderly, not an easy task for a six year old who is just learning to control a pencil. For this reason children are given the opportunity to express their findings in many different ways, many of them not traditional.

But to appreciate fully the changes that have occurred in the past twenty years, it is necessary to turn our attention to their impact in the classroom.

For the lower age groups (five to eight) there is often a multiplicity of structure apparatus (such as Stern, Cuisinaire and Unifix), equipment for weighing and measuring and containers for extending understanding of capacity and volume. In such an environment learning will be active rather than passive and children will be presented with mathematical ideas in a wide variety of ways. The emphasis of the programme that is followed (whether teacher-led or book-based) will tend to be investigative and, if such a programme is to succeed, the children will be encouraged to talk. Language is an integral part of number work, for words both indicate the level of perception a child has reached and enable him to verbalize his findings. The vocabulary so gained does not simply represent the acquisition of purely abstract mathematical terms. Expressions such as 'more than', 'less than', 'greater than', 'smaller than', 'half of', 'is double', 'can be divided by', are invariably mastered before more complex terms (such as 'transformation' or 'approximation').

The findings (or discoveries) of the children will reflect this interest in language. Often work will be displayed in an accepted mathematical form, such as a graph, and be accompanied by a description of how the information was collected and ordered and why a particular method was chosen to present it. These displays will indicate something of the range of activities that young children undertake. Some children may be classifying objects into size, shape or colour, others may be discovering equalities and inequalities, others will be mastering mathematical operations, or coming to some understanding of such things as conservation or transformation.

And here in my list of objectives we come once again to the basic problem that we always have to face when dealing with something as abstract as number: terminology. To help a child to understand invariance (or conservation) a teacher may simply provide sand and a range of containers, or a water tray and a variety of bottles. The child will discover that a pint of water remains a pint of water whatever shape it is contained in, but like as not he will present this 'learning' as playing and perhaps observe to his mother that he did no maths in school today.

This use of practical activity to extend mathematical experience and the development of a language of mathematics continues throughout the years of a child's primary school life. The use of apparatus, whether simple counters or an elaborate box of coloured rods, helps children to understand the nature of calculations. They should be regarded as aids in the transition to formal work (the child's eventual goal). It is to be hoped, of course, that the use of some types of apparatus will also enable children to pursue their studies more quickly and at a deeper level. The advent of the electronic calculator has taken out of mathematics the need for time-consuming arithmetical calculations. Indeed the modern calculator is but one of a long line of aids – the abacus, Napiers Bones and the slide rule can hardly be described as new inventions. Again we have to resolve a dilemma. As a teacher I can well support the observation that ideas are more important than mechanical processes and that a child using a calculator properly has control of both operation and material. But as a parent should I not be worried if, without a calculator (or some other aid), my daughter cannot solve $120 \div 10$?

It is in an attempt to dispel this disquiet and to further children's understanding of the nature of number that considerable efforts are made to present ideas in as many ways as possible. Consider, for example, some methods of solving the sum 19×41.

19×41

$$
\begin{array}{rl}
10 \times 41 = & 410 \\
9 \times 41 = & 369+ \\
\hline
& 779
\end{array}
$$

or

19×41

$$
\begin{array}{rl}
19 \times 40 = & 760 \\
19 \times 1 = & 19+ \\
\hline
& 779
\end{array}
$$

or

19×41

$$
\begin{array}{rl}
10 \times 40 = & 400 \\
9 \times 40 = & 360 \\
10 \times 1 = & 10 \\
9 \times 1 = & 9+ \\
\hline
& 779
\end{array}
$$

or

19×41

$$
\begin{array}{r}
41 \times \\
19 \\
\hline
410 \\
369 + \\
\hline
779 \\
\hline
\end{array}
\qquad
\begin{array}{r}
19 \times \\
41 \\
\hline
760 \\
19 + \\
\hline
779 \\
\hline
\end{array}
$$

or

19×41

$$
\begin{array}{l}
20 \times 41 = 820 \\
1 \times 41 = 41 - \\
\hline
779 \\
\hline
\end{array}
$$

or

19×41 ('Russian peasant' method)

$$
\begin{array}{ll}
19 \times 41 & 41 \\
9 \times 82 & 82 \\
4 \times 164 & 656 + \\
2 \times 328 & 779 \\
1 \times 656 & \\
\end{array}
$$

The observation that children derive more benefit from doing one sum five ways than five sums one way is not as banal as it might at first sight appear. The whole purpose of such activities is to establish in children's minds the nature of number, that mathematics is a study of relationships and patterns, that precision is essential.

The changed approach to primary school mathematics has resulted in a much broader curriculum than that which was followed twenty years ago. The four rules are still taught and applied, but without the excessive emphasis upon drill and technique. Such things as simple statistics, positive and negative numbers, the properties of cubes, cuboids and cylinders, symmetry, reflection, approximation, square and cube numbers, topology, area, capacity and volume are now taught in the majority of schools.

The dangers inherent in this widening of the curriculum and our increased expectation of children need not be spelt out in detail. Children still need to know their tables (as well as understand them); they need regular practice if computation skills are to be retained. It is of little value if they know about Euler and Descartes, but have forgotten how to divide 37 by 3 or multiply 16 by 5. There have been schools where these new freedoms have been abused and the teacher, instead of being a provoker of thought, has lost herself in a welter of graphs, mathematical models, click wheels and good intentions.

In evaluating the place of mathematics in the primary school we need to ask whether the activities (both practical or textbook-based) enable children to interpret their environment, to cope with number as it impinges upon their ordinary everyday life, and whether they give them some understanding of mathematical structure by helping them to master basic principles and a knowledge of how to apply them.

The organization of mathematics teaching varies from school to school throughout the country. In some schools specialization has led to the establishment of maths laboratories, in others the adoption of a particular scheme (such as the 'Fletcher series') has led to a complete reappraisal of the content and direction of the mathematics syllabus.

The final judgement on how successful these new approaches have been cannot be made in the immediate future. The children who have been most exposed to them have not yet reached the stage at which we can adequately measure the extent to which understanding has been given to number, meaning to abstractions.

It would be easy, of course, to apply outdated tests to measure progress but any results would be of little value. Today few children of primary school age could reduce 2 miles, 5 furlongs, 1 chain, 2 yards to feet – the sort of activity which filled many an hour of my own school days. But then, had I at nine years old been asked to express 7 in base 2, I would have been equally at a loss.

7 Environmental Studies

William Cobbett, the nineteenth-century writer on rural affairs, was not in favour of public education. In *Advice to Young Men* (published in 1830) he suggested that schools were poor places for children because their teaching was devitalized and unrelated to living, that although 'book drill' might do little harm it certainly did very little good. Cobbett, somewhat idealistically, contrasted school *teaching* with the *learning* his own children achieved as they worked on his rural holding. His eldest son, he records, was amazed at the size of a crop of melons that the holding had produced. Cobbett referred his son to a book on melon cultivation, the instructions of which he had followed from the planting of the seed to the harvesting of the crop. On hearing this his son read the same book 'perhaps twenty times over'. Similarly Cobbett records that arithmetic was learned because 'calculations about farming affairs forced arithmetic upon us; the use, the necessity of the thing led us to the study'.

Of course it would be unrealistic to regard *Advice to Young Men* as anything more than an interesting view of the education scene in the nineteenth century. But the principle – that children learn most effectively when they are closely and realistically involved in a study – is at the root of the curriculum changes that have occurred in primary education over the past thirty years.

The involvement with the study of real things and learning from actual (rather than vicarious) experience has, of course, always been a characteristic of children. The pre-school child drinks in experience, grabs at it and stores it away, often to reveal it in the future in the most unexpected way. The knowledge so gained is haphazard, unrelated to conventional subject areas and coloured by personal experience. In Chapter 5 I made the point that personal vision reveals itself in children's writings.

In a similar way the young child tends to marry together the significant and the inconsequential in a bizarre, disarming manner. 'Yes,' replied a four year old when asked about a family outing. 'I remember the castle. Grandma broke her teeth on a sandwich and I dropped a penny down the well.' Would the castle have been remembered but for Grandma's discomfiture, and did this in turn help recall the well?

As adults we can never really pinpoint what it is that gives meaning to words, comprehensibility to the experience with which we bombard our young people. For many years infant school teachers have realized that children learn best when information is presented to them in a way which ignores traditional subject barriers. A wheel brought into the classroom might lead to a discussion about the first wheels (history), research into the nature of a wheel (mathematics), the function of a wheel (science), the use of wheeled vehicles (history, geography) and the poetry of wheels in words and music (literature, music). At the end of the study – which might take a week or a month to complete – each child's knowledge and understanding of wheels will be that much greater. Hopefully each person in the classroom (including the teacher) will have increased his appreciation of what makes a wheel significant for him as an individual and for society at large. But this point needs to be stressed. The good teacher will not be aiming at giving each child identical experience. If this were so she would not be far removed from the payment-by-results philosophy I touched upon in Chapter 4. It is important to remember that the degree to which children understand the context of any lesson, formal or informal, will depend upon the extent to which basic concepts have been grasped. Is there any point, for example, in teaching 'cave men' to seven year olds as the beginning of a study of developmental history? A seven year old has little understanding of time (let alone man's drive for food, shelter and sex, which are the basic ingredients of a cave economy). History may be the study of yesterday, but for young children the yesterdays need to be yesterdays they can grasp – like their mother's childhood, their Grandma's kitchen.

This is not to say that the early years of schooling are unstructured and teachers simply wait for children to announce their interests or bring in odds and ends for the teacher to take as a 'centre of interest' and build upon.

The task of the teacher is also to introduce materials (tactile and visual) for children to use, study and comment upon. There are few infant classrooms which do not contain displays to interest the children – fabrics, coins, dolls, bones, books, pictures, pots, every conceivable kind of artefact. Such displays may mark the starting point for studies which the children are making as individuals, in small groups or as a whole class. On the other hand they may mark the culmination of an experience in which all have shared.

Many studies will begin outside the school. With infants this may involve a walk down the streets in which they themselves live – and this should be much more a learning experience than sitting, desk-bound, listening to teachers talk. A hole in the road, the houses, the shops, the people they pass, the names of the streets, the sounds and smells of the area are, for the gifted teacher, the beginning of environmental studies. Such studies will have scant regard for the niceties of traditional academic disciplines. There will be a blurring of boundaries between mathematics, English, science, geography and history. But when, on their return to school, the children search for further information they will become aware that arbitrary divisions do exist. Slowly they will be led to discriminate, to present their mathematical findings in a mathematical form (a graph as well as a sentence, for instance), to group together similar subject areas so that the ideas they present are sequential and related. They will also be regularly reminded that there are many different ways to record and present information – by drawing, by writing, by speaking, by using a camera or a tape recorder, by preparing a play, through puppetry. They will inevitably make books, although books (individual or group) will not be presented as the only acceptable way of recording and presenting the information which has been acquired.

As the child grows older and moves into the middle years of

schooling the places visited and the topics attempted will grow increasingly complex and be much wider ranging. The young child learns in his home, his family and his immediate environment and this learning through experience is immediately extended when he enters school. As he develops, physically, emotionally and intellectually, the ways of learning are applied against an ever-widening canvas. A seven year old is shown how to make a study of the streets near his home. At ten years of age he might well be expected to attempt a similar exercise while on a school journey in quite a different part of the country. What information do I need to acquire? How can I acquire it? Where can I go to find out? What resources are there available to me – books, museums, maps, art galleries, people? The approach is the same as that he used when he was seven, but the level of response will be much more developed. There should be greater awareness and observation, a keener brain, a developed perception.

As the child matures he will also begin to understand something of the nature of the different disciplines that a study of the environment involves. There is a way of working if the problem to be solved has its roots in history. There are strategies which, if correctly followed, will enable scientific experiments to be carried out effectively and successfully. There are questions which geographers ask, the answers to which will help them in their particular study. Teachers of children in the eight to twelve age range will therefore be helping children to come to terms with specialism and they will build into their programmes ways of looking, discovering and recording which reflect this growing maturity.

The whole concept of environmental studies and a project approach to learning is based upon our knowledge of how children learn. They learn by experiencing, by doing, by involving all their senses. If modern approaches to curriculum development can be seen in this way, the apparent diffuseness of the curriculum should not cause undue concern. Because the 'History of the Saxon Kingdoms' does not appear on the junior syllabus it does not mean that Saxon England will be ignored.

Because the teacher in John's class seems to concentrate upon pond life to the exclusion of geographical and historical topics it does not inevitably mean that John will leave the school unaware of Elizabeth I and with a scant knowledge of glaciers and moraines. He will meet other teachers who will present him with other areas of study (even assuming, as is most unlikely, that John's teacher remains pond-bound for four years and that John stays pond-bound with him). But take this example further: apart from the basic skills of reading and writing, and the ability to cope with numbers, what facts are there that children *have* to know before they are eleven? How many facts can you remember from your primary school days? What is of far greater concern, I would suggest, is the methods we employ in teaching children how to acquire facts when they need them. The *how* in the process of education at this stage is far more important than the *what*.

Throughout this book I have stressed that young children learn best when they are deeply and personally involved in the learning process. For many schools environmental studies are based upon local resources – buildings (like the church), places (the village and the town), collections (museums and art galleries), the immediate area around the school (industrial wasteland or beech woods). This local experience is often extended by visits to places further afield. These visits may last for a day, a week or even a fortnight. Often the costs of such trips are met from a combination of public and private funds (the local authority allowing some public money to be spent on visits, with parents' contributions meeting the rest).

School journeys, which are now very much part of the primary school experience, provide an example of how learning outside school gives reality and purpose to work undertaken within it. A trip lasting three days is arranged in a canal boat. The children are prepared for the experience by some 'lead-in lessons', often very formal in content and presentation, on the canal builders. They learn about the mechanics of lock gates, they study their proposed route, they determine how they will record their experiences. They will be shown film strips, listen to radio programmes and watch television presentations.

The journey itself will confirm the book knowledge, give it relevance and meaning and extend it. Actually going through a tunnel cut by navvies through solid rock is quite a different experience from reading about it in a book. But the journey will do something else. It will create new centres of interest, new starting points quite unrelated to canals. The children will make notes on all that happens (from the quality of breakfast to feeding the swans), they will take photographs (to be developed in school as part of their science programme), they will record in words, in pencil sketch, in oil pastel drawing, on tape recorder – and in their minds. For much that they have learned will never be put down in a way that we, the adults in their lives, can measure and classify.

On returning to school the experience is further extended by written work, by picture and model making, by discussion, by a visit to a canal museum, by research into books and by the presentation of all that has been learned to the whole school community. This may take the form of displays of work, slide shows and assemblies.

It may seem odd that I include assemblies, which began as acts of corporate worship, in this chapter of the book. I make no excuse for doing so. In my opinion assemblies are, and have always been, about the sharing of common experiences. One of the common experiences of man could be described as 'spiritual', the revelation and sharing of certain truths to all who participate. The traditional assembly – of Bible reading, hymn and prayer taken by the head or senior teacher – no longer seems to meet the needs of our time. All children are expected to assemble for worship five times per week, yet only 9 per cent * of adults in England attend a place of worship on Sundays. But the falling away of formal worship in school assemblies has in no way reduced their significance. In my opinion it has enhanced them. Children and teachers are now able to share mutual interests. The 'coming together' is now much more likely to focus upon written work well spoken, paintings well

* Although 18 per cent of the adult population actively support a religious order (1977 Gallup Poll findings).

displayed and playlets conceived by the children to explain their researches than it is upon trivial misdemeanours and sports results. In this way the more secular assembly is fulfilling the very real need for a time in school when ideas, aspirations, ideals and hopes can be shared by all.

In assemblies led by children we are able to see and present the school as a community of children who can learn from the examples that they themselves set. Older children prepare material for their peers and for their younger brothers and sisters. Younger children prepare material for children of their own age and yet are able to share it with those much older than themselves. From such sharings there comes tolerance, an understanding of the pace of living and learning of their fellows, an awareness that a school is a community which has at its root a common and definable purpose.

Such assemblies, of course, do not deliberately exclude prayer. I have heard children thank God for the life of Mohamet, the stories of Aesop and the poetry of de la Mare. I have seen Jewish children take part in plays about the Knights of St John and heard Moslem children read poems about the Nativity of Christ.

Assemblies are often focal points in the day which is why many schools now hold them in the middle of the morning rather than (as used to be the case) at the beginning of school. I believe that in attending an assembly a visitor to a school can learn much about its beliefs and much about the quality of its work. Often a ragged, noisy, disjointed, adult-dominated assembly is indicative of a school under stress, a school looking for direction and purpose – direction, let me hasten to add, that will not come simply by a return to the statutory hymn, prayer and reading of my childhood. It would be appropriate to observe here, however, that schools supported by religious organizations would have a somewhat different emphasis. Children would be engaged in leading assemblies, but these assemblies would undoubtedly contain an element of sectarian teaching.

Environmental studies shared by the whole school, through displays of work and assemblies will be further supported by work in music and drama, to which I now turn my attention.

8 The Arts

It has been said that the young child plays with materials and thereby learns them. The truth of this observation can nowhere be seen as clearly as in the field of the arts – picture-making, modelling, music and drama. The first scribble of childhood with a well-sucked crayon will as surely lead to the making of recognizable shapes to represent 'Mummy' as will his early enthusiastic claps to the rhythm of nursery rhyme or popular song to the free-flowing steps of a yet unknown pop culture or the formal patterns of the traditional dance. There seems to be in all young children a desire to express themselves by making marks and constructions, by making sounds and through physical response to the sounds that they hear.

Indeed it could be argued that it is largely as a result of man's preoccupation with these elements of his make-up that he has been able to dominate the world. From earliest time man has made marks to decorate the walls of his dwellings, has cut patterns into his tools, chiselled designs into stone, coloured his earthenware pots. His progress towards civilization has been marked by the ability he has shown in the adaptation of his environment – by building in stone, brick and wood, by spinning and weaving, by working in metal.

With the passing of time, the arts have become so inextricably woven into our daily lives that we tend to take them for granted and ignore the central place that they have always occupied in the human being. As a headteacher I am sometimes confronted by a parent who sees the education process purely in terms of the manipulation of numbers, the mastery of spelling and solid progress through a reading primer.

It seems to me that in this area we in the Western world have lost our way. Our means of production have become so specialized that we have lost sight of the fact that the quality of life cannot be simply measured by the size of the pay packet, holidays overseas or the performance and elegance of the family car. The things we buy for our homes, the tools we use in the factory and in the kitchen, have to be conceived, designed, made. We need people who have a feeling for materials and yet we deny young children the time to discover their nature.

This division is merely a reflection of the society outside school. Most capital cities have specially built complexes for the arts, staffed by highly paid experts in theatre, music, painting and sculpture. The culture-complex is a way, I suppose, of surrogating our responsibilities. We are not denying the arts a place, even though we are insulating them from the everyday life of the majority of our people. Contrast this with many a third world country, where market places are filled with the products of local craftsmen, products for everyday use rather than for the currency of the tourist.

Over the years the primary school has gone some way to correcting this imbalance. In doing so, teachers have been occasionally accused of devoting more time to painting and junk modelling than to the more conventional areas of the curriculum. The momentum towards strengthening the arts content in the curriculum began in the 1920s. In Vienna, Franz Cizek had convincingly demonstrated that young children were artists, that their paintings and drawings showed insight as well as technical skill. His work was not unnoticed and the publicity which he received certainly helped educationalists in other countries who believed that the arts should play a central part in the school life of young children.

In England the effect of the work of Marion Richardson, an inspector of art for the London County Council, was profound. She began a revolution so fundamental in the theory and practice of art teaching that the impact of her thinking lives on long after her death.

But what evidence is there in English schools to substantiate this observation? On what grounds should the arts be considered as central to the curriculum? To answer these questions we need to examine the kinds of experience which teachers provide for young children.

First and foremost the classroom is seen as a workshop which contains a wide range of tactile materials for children to use. Paint, dyes, crayons, pastels, chalks and pencils are commonly used for colouring, but the way that these materials are applied is of far greater significance. Paint does not *have* to be applied by brush – it could be applied equally well by sponge, or stick, or lino roller (brayer) or finger tip. Dyes are not only suitable for use on fabric, they can be applied by brush over wax pictures to produce resists, applied by spray to give texture to models made in papier-mâché or plaster. Paper for picture-making does not have to be white or grey; it can be textured and coloured. Thus the materials that are provided for children to use may be conventional, but the good teacher will be helping her class to experiment with them so that each child will come to understand something of their properties – that dye is suitable for one technique, but poor for another, that one paper gives an excellent surface for lino block printing, but is unsuitable for chalk drawings or ink sketches.

As knowledge of materials develops, so does the child's awareness of his particular strengths and weaknesses. For one child working in paint on large sheets of paper may be, for her, the most satisfying activity of the school week. For another child printing has particular fascination, for a third constructions in paper, card and wire. To make each child 'do' each activity for the sake of administrative convenience accomplishes little. It diminishes the value of the particular gifts that each child has to offer and prevents the further development of those skills which set her apart from her peers. The perceptive teacher will seek to broaden children's experience, to widen their horizons. At what stage should Janet, who paints well in powder colour, be introduced to water colours, acrylics and oils? Should John be shown how to use an electric soldering iron now that he has demonstrated his ability and skill in model making with galvanized wire?

Awareness of the nature of materials – that clay is pliable

when prepared in a certain way, that wood is hard, that PVA adhesives have different properties from cellulose paste and impact glues – will lead to further discovery. 'How do I?' 'What should I use?' Questions such as these refer not only to the properties of the materials but also to the correct way in which they should be handled. Has Peter's clay gone hard because he stored it incorrectly? Did his pot fracture in firing because he prepared the clay badly? Is there a way of stopping the dye from running when the fabric is washed?

The answers to these problems lead towards a very real understanding of the nature of craft work, for the problems posed are as old as mankind itself. The teacher will not just be giving her children experience in traditional crafts, she will also be bringing the children face to face with the problems they pose and helping them to solve them. This will involve the mastery of skills, the use of specialist equipment, the practice which is often the forerunner of perfection. From playing with materials to using them for a purpose is a process that occurs throughout the primary years, and continues beyond them into adolescence and into adult life.

The arts are not presented in isolation, as a thing apart from the rest of life. The primary school is perhaps the only place where the arts are used successfully to comment upon and give meaning to the whole of the child's experience. Visually the classroom, the corridors, the hall, are exciting places, with children's pictures and displays of photographs, models, artefacts and books giving meaning and purpose to their writings. 'We went, we saw, we felt, and if you (child, adult, teacher, visitor) are sufficiently interested, you too can learn what we discovered.'

It is often a worthwhile exercise, when visiting a school, to notice how much these displays tell us of the development of children in the years five to eleven. Pictures painted by the youngest children often contain imagery. A round yellow shape entitled 'Mum' could just as well fit under the neighbouring painting entitled 'flower'. In doing, the child grows and learns; the value of the activity lies in placing the yellow paint on the paper in a way determined by the child alone – not in the finished picture (which is more often given a title to placate adults than for any other reason). As the child matures, imagery gives way to reality. The lines, shapes and patterns are placed in such a way as to communicate and to enable another person to understand.

This intellectual growth is accompanied by a flowering of visual awareness, by an acceptance of the disciplines which all crafts impose. These disciplines are often ignored by those who devalue the place of the arts in the curriculum and, therefore, merit consideration here. In giving children the opportunity to explore a range of materials, teachers are also allowing children to choose. Having chosen, however, options for action become somewhat limited. If chalk is to be carved, what precautions need to be taken to protect the area in which it is worked, what tools will be required, what technique is appropriate to chalk, what can chalk be used for that is peculiar to that medium? The young craftsman will need to work within the restraints imposed by the materials and the skill he has in using particular and specialized tools, and also within the time that is made available to him. Are these restraints very different from those we experience in the adult world and is it surprising that we should find them exercising their influence within a classroom of young children? It is through pressures such as these (and their resolution) that the child grows. There never seems to be enough time in a classroom to set up a loom, to finish a painting, to complete a piece of embroidery, to prepare, use and clean a silk screen. Perhaps it is because a multitude of decisions have to be taken, each related to the activities undertaken by children as individuals or as members of small groups, that the visitor to a classroom gains the impression that primary school teaching is very unorganized, free, ill-disciplined. In fact the reverse is true. It is only by defining the framework within which children work, by continually reassessing the activities being undertaken, and having the ability to relate tomorrow's programme to today's progress that the primary school teacher can work in the way I have described.

The pattern I have outlined for the visual arts applies also to music. Music-making has developed on two broad fronts, singing and instrumental. The teaching of singing and of notation and rhythm has long been a characteristic of schools and I propose to devote little space to it here. Suffice it to say that the songs which children learn are now more varied, more international and less stuffy than when I first started teaching. 'Nymphs and Shepherds' might still be included in the repertory of some schools, but songs from the West Indies, Europe, America and Asia have brought school song books more into line with the fast-moving rhythms of contemporary culture than hitherto.

It is the development of instrumental teaching, however, that we need to consider here. In introducing children to music-making it is appropriate that they should begin by making sounds. The simplest way of making sounds, apart from using the voice, is to tap and to bang. An exploration of sound patterns (rhythms built up with percussion instruments such as cymbal, drum, wood block, shaker, tambour, triangle) helps children to begin to discriminate: quiet sounds, noisy sounds, continuous sounds which emerge only to die away, sounds which have a regular beat, sounds which are instant upon the ear and sounds which linger as they fade into silence.

These elements were included in the percussion band which was dear to the heart of many an infant headmistress in the 1930s. They help adults to identify the child with a feeling for music, giving a valuable starting point but little more.

Since the last war the development of music in primary schools has owed much to the specialist teacher, the trained musician who can seize upon a child's natural musical ability and develop it to the full. More and more children are benefiting from such specialized teaching and it is not uncommon to find ten year olds who are competent performers on violin, cello, flute, clarinet, oboe or guitar. The extent of specialist instrumental teaching varies from district to district. Some local authorities actively encourage young musicians, others merely note that a school is spending a percentage of its capitation on music but do little to further it by giving additional support.

Between singing and basic percussion and the sophistication of instrumental teaching by visiting peripatetic teachers lies a broad band of children whose knowledge of music is being extended by their own class teacher through the descant recorder. Many children in the seven to eleven age range now play this instrument, the more capable being introduced to the treble and tenor recorder. In schools where the recorder is used extensively, ensembles are often formed so that children can be introduced to such things as harmony and to follow the directions of a conductor. More important, however, than the quality of the sound produced is all that is learned from the act of playing together. Discipline in such an activity is not, cannot, be imposed from without. The very act of corporate music-making creates tensions from which responsibility springs and flowers.

Music-making is difficult to separate from dance, for one supports the other. Traditional dance, Morris, for example and folk dance are commonly taught in most schools and some teachers have also begun to teach ballroom dancing to nine and ten year olds.

'Free' or 'creative dance' is another area where music and drama combine. Here, however, the emphasis tends to be upon expressive body movement – to tell a story, express an emotion, mime a process, explore an idea. Often these 'movement' lessons are linked to other areas of the curriculum. For example, a group of nine year olds might be investigating witchcraft in medieval England. They will have discovered something of the folk lore of witches, perhaps listened to some music based upon a legend (Berlioz's 'Witches' Sabbath' perhaps), read the story of Snow White, and heard some poems about cats and bats and spirits of the night. But, before they themselves try to create a witch in paint, in clay or in words, the teacher will help them to explore the subject with their own bodies. How might she move? How would she look when she cast her spell? How would she respond to kindness and goodness? How would she feel when confronted with a power greater than her own? How can we as a group build up a story around good and evil that other people would understand? The writing and the painting which comes from such a shared experience is, invariably, of a far higher quality than would be the case if such joint exploration had not taken place.

As with all the aspects of curriculum that I have touched upon, these 'movement' lessons * involve individual as well as group response. Sometimes the direction that the activity follows is determined by a rhythm beaten out by a teacher or a child upon a tambour or a drum, at others it follows sounds made by the human voice, or is built upon a piece of recorded music. On some occasions there is a clear aim (to give additional meaning to a topic), at other times the activity is largely spontaneous, and will itself become the starting point for picture-making and story-writing.

I would argue, however, that their importance in the lives of young people goes far beyond the perceived, the measurable, the expected. The occasional visit to the theatre, museum, art gallery or concert is not enough. For young children such experiences should be regular occurrences, times when the arts they themselves are involved in are seen against a wider canvas, when book learning is presented within a context that children can understand. To organize such visits presents obvious difficulties, particularly for children living in a rural community. There are schools, usually in large cities, which have resources where much progress has been made, but even in London, Birmingham, York, Chester or Liverpool much still needs to be done to awaken teachers and parents to the richness of the cultural heritage which is lying untapped.

* 'Movement' lessons are regarded as part of the physical education curriculum. It supplements, but does not replace, traditional activities in the gym – skills with balls, hoops and ropes, team games and swimming.

9 Other Curriculum Areas

We have examined, in some detail, those aspects of the curriculum which occupy a central place in the life and work of a school. However, the 'core' I have outlined has omitted a number of subject areas which are common to most schools.

In the opinion of some readers the first of these, religious education, might deserve more space than I feel able to give it. In the years since the war the place that religious education occupies as the 'Fourth R' in the curriculum has been questioned. The Hadow Report on primary education was able to observe that 'The teaching of religion is at the heart of all teaching. An education which leaves this instinct without acknowledgement must be defective, starving a child of a most important side of his nature.' The Plowden Committee were unable to present such a united front. The majority of the committee were in favour of religious education retaining its place as the one compulsory subject in the curriculum. A minority of its members, however, believed that religious education should not figure in the curriculum at all.*

The change of attitude, which is clearly reflected in these two reports, is not surprising. Our churches are not as full now as they were at the turn of the century; immigrant communities have brought with them their own religious beliefs and practices.†

* 'In our view the root of the trouble is that religious education is bound to involve theology: and theology is both too recondite and too controversial a subject to be suitable for inclusion in the curriculum of primary schools. It cannot be properly adapted either to the understanding of children of this age or to the methods by which we are proposing that they should be taught' (note of reservation on religious education, Plowden Report).

† For example, in 1970 the Muslim community numbered 250,000. By 1977 it had grown to 400,000. Plowden stressed the need for an under-

The validity of the Christian ethic has come under detailed scrutiny. Against this crumbling support for organized religion must be set the fact that England is still nominally a Christian country with Church and state inextricably intertwined. While few parents (if my experience is anything to go by) wish for religious education of a denominational nature to play a central part in the life of a school, even fewer express a desire for it to be removed entirely from the curriculum.

To some extent the dilemma was resolved by the 1944 Education Act. This Act improved the financial position of voluntary schools, of which there are two main categories, aided and controlled. In aided schools all religious education may be denominational; in controlled schools there must be provision for not more than two periods of denominational instruction each week for children whose parents desire it. Most voluntary schools are Church of England, but there are a substantial number which are Roman Catholic, Jewish, Methodist and undenominational Christian. The weakness of this provision, however, lies in the spread of these schools across the country. Many voluntary schools were founded in the wake of government intervention in education in the 1860 to 1890s and the siting of Church schools today has little relationship to local Church membership. This means that many parents do not have a choice of voluntary or state school. If they live in a village which has only one school and that school is supported by a Church, to that school their child will go.

But, as in all things educational, there is compromise. Parents have the right to withdraw their children from RE lessons, as well as from acts of corporate worship. However, whereas these particular regulations were easy to implement when RE lessons were clearly defined on a timetable and the act of worship had a definite Christian content, they are now much more difficult to interpret when religious education has become part of an

---

standing of world religions. 'Care should be taken to include, sympathetically, those who represent non-Christian tradition, Saladin for example, as well as St Bernard.'

integrated curriculum. Let me clarify this with an example. In the past, the life and work of Rahere, founder of St Bartholomew's Hospital in London, could have been presented as part of the religious education syllabus. Here is a man who, moved by the Holy Spirit at a time of personal crisis, left his comfortable life at the court of Henry I to dedicate the remainder of his days to the poor, the sick and the dying. Undoubtedly a good story with a number of unequivocal and very acceptable points to help develop the children's understanding of Christ at work in the contemporary world. However, should this story be presented as part of a larger study of medieval life, how can parents withdraw their children on religious grounds (assuming they wish to do so)?

The Churches have long been aware of this sort of problem. After the last war 'agreed syllabuses' were produced by most education authorities for use in their schools, and this practice continues to the present time. Today the agreed syllabus gives great flexibility of approach, so that most teachers can find something in it which they can teach without too great a straining of their consciences. The effect of this has been to produce something of a rag bag of ideas, a syllabus to cover topics as varied as smoking, colour prejudice, world religions, thoughtfulness for others, sexual equality and stealing.

This suggests that the provisions for religious education implicit in the 1944 Act have been overtaken by events. Perhaps if the phrase 'religious education' were used instead of 'religious instruction' the situation would be less confused. Personally I doubt it. The Church of England's Education Board seem to have accepted the need for a complete change in the law, which itself represents a considerable move from the position adopted by Archbishop William Temple who, speaking on the 1944 Bill, observed, 'I think teachers are a little liable to ignore the fact that whereas it is objectionable to force the teachers to conduct prayers against their consciences, it also is objectionable to force the children to omit prayers for the sake of their teachers' consciences.'

The 1944 Act of course, merely confirmed the exceptional

and central place that religious instruction had always occupied in English education. It stemmed from the belief that one of the principal tasks of schools was to mould character and to develop moral values. These virtues, it was thought, stemmed from an acceptance of the Christian ethic. 'Schools,' according to Joseph Lancaster, 'were places where large numbers will be living in His [God's] fear, in the knowledge of His ways and in the daily remembrance of His commandments.' Bishop Philpotts of Exeter went even further: 'The context is not whether the children of the poor shall be taught, but whether Papists, Unitarians ... Socialists shall henceforth be recognized as having a legal right to an equal distribution of the privilege of educating and being paid for educating the rising generations of Englishmen.' *

Tradition in England dies hard. Teachers like to feel that the climate in the schools in which they work helps children to 'acquire' moral values, and they go about achieving this in a variety of ways. What a good school does – and does continually – is to stress the place of the individual in society, and the fact that to care for others is of paramount importance. This care should permeate everything that happens in school – care for other people's property, care for the school fabric, care for the weaker, the younger, the less gifted, the physically handicapped, the immature. This caring will not be confined to the emotions, but be manifest in many practical ways. Some schools, for example, attempt fully to integrate handicapped children into their programme; others have firmly established links with old people's homes and national children's charities, which open up direct and close association between child and pensioner, child and child.

The projection of the school as a caring community is not an aspect of the curriculum that can be evaluated at a glance. All that goes on within it that confirms the children's feelings and attitudes and deepens their sympathy and understanding about relationships and the worth of people as individuals is, in my opinion, a central part of the school's function. This has been

*The Heart of the Matter, 1839.

described as the hidden curriculum of a school, but is this what is *really* meant by religious education?

It seems to me that we have carried with us, into a secular age, the trappings of a religious past. These trappings exist in many aspects of our society, of which our schools are one. Teachers might think that they are able to influence children's moral development. Equally Parliamentarians and Church leaders might believe that schools are places where spirituality emerges and is fostered. The influence of school, however, is not all-pervasive, for the impact of television, attitudes within the home, the values of the peer group, are of far greater significance and are much longer lasting.

Perhaps the time has come for our schools to be relieved of the responsibility for religious education and to concentrate upon things that teachers are equipped to teach. I do not think that this will result in schools ignoring the spiritual development of their pupils, for this can be fostered without recourse to sectarian postures and beliefs.

A second curriculum area I have largely ignored is that of physical education. And yet its inclusion here, following hard upon spiritual education, is not as inappropriate as might first appear.

Physical education was introduced into schools in the early 1900s, when evidence (mainly obtained at the medical examination of recruits for the army to fight in the South African wars) suggested that many children were unhealthy and physically undeveloped. From such beginnings has grown an exciting and realistic programme of physical education, the limits of which have not been reached. Children at primary schools are being introduced to an ever-expanding list of activities. The football, netball, cricket and rounders of my school days continue as a central part of the programme, but to them have been added gymnastics, life-saving, swimming for personal survival, stool ball, volley ball, athletics, table tennis and judo. The aim has not been to foster one or two team games, but to present children with a variety of physical challenges in the belief that through an exploration of a range of activities each child will discover his own abilities, his own strengths.

Within such a climate the school team – and the competitions it enters – may survive. But if children's interests in physical education are widely spread, failure on the football field is not so acutely felt, and the elevation of members of the team at moments of triumph becomes less significant in the day-to-day life of the school.

Examine this under the umbrella of the hidden curriculum. If the life of a school is distorted by a desire to do well in competitive games what does this tell us about the nature of that school and of the adults that run it? As an English international coach remarked after the national team had failed to secure a place in the 1978 World Cup finals, 'If we have mothers and fathers standing on the side lines screaming at their nine year olds to "take out" an opponent by fair means or foul, what hope is there for young people to play games in the right spirit, for enthusiasm, for fun?'

It is interesting that in Eastern Europe physical education plays a much more central part in the life and direction of schools than it does in England. In Yugoslavia, for example, the schools (by Western standards) are poorly equipped. The only exception is in the sophisticated and extensive provision that is made for physical education. By the direction of scarce resources into physical culture, by insisting that the staff appointed to use the equipment so provided are of the highest possible standard, the children are shown where their priorities should lie.

A third subject area which often finds itself submerged within an integrated programme is housecraft or home economics. This is a somewhat grand title for a very basic activity, cooking. Most children, before they come to school, help their mothers in the everyday life of the home. They go to the shops, buy food, help prepare food, lay the table, eat the meals they themselves have prepared and (hopefully) clear away afterwards.

This pattern is continued in many schools. In the school in which I work, for example, five and six year olds, working under the direction of an infant helper, will be taken to buy ingredients for biscuits or cakes. These ingredients will then be prepared – and this will involve reading a recipe (English) and weighing (mathematics). The food is then cooked in the children's electric cooker and taken home.

Older children cook at a more sophisticated level than this. I have known some eight and nine year olds who have prepared their own school lunch; others who have linked their cooking to project work they were undertaking on countries of the European community; and yet another group who went for one morning a week to a college of further education where they learned from housecraft students something of the nature of food, of carbohydrates, protein, fats, vitamins and roughage.

It is apparent, from this list, that housecraft will inevitably take the teacher into the whole area of health and the nature of the human being. Try as we might, it is very difficult to keep personal viewpoints and moral judgements out of our answers to many of the questions children ask during discussions on health. If it's wrong to smoke, why does the vicar do it? Is drinking bad for you? However these questions are answered, they will present a problem in the minds of some of the children taking part. If the nurse who came to school *really knows* that smoking can affect the life of an unborn child, what about my Mum who smokes like a chimney and is pregnant? What are drugs, and why is it that my teacher always seems to avoid answering my questions about them? Of course for the teacher who is fearful of offending a parent or of upsetting a child a non-committal response is the easiest way out, which is perhaps why the debate on sex education continues unresolved. Some primary teachers avoid sex education on the grounds that sex is such an emotionally charged subject that it can adequately be dealt with only at home. On the other hand some teachers believe that at about nine years old children are able to learn about the functional nature of human sexual activity without the embarrassment which might come with adolescence and that to have some understanding of sexuality is important before the tensions of the early teens confuse and bedevil the subject.

There is one other reason for an increasing concern. The primary school can no longer ignore puberty – more and more girls are beginning their periods before their twelfth birthday. To cope with the stress that growing-up can bring, children need understanding and sympathy, support from the adults around them and the security that this gives. If our response is perceptive, they will begin to know something of the integrity which should underpin all human relationships, that it is in wholeness that personality develops and grows and that such wholeness cannot be judged purely in terms of academic performance, skill at games, success with paint and clay or in the sexual role play which has prevented many a woman from fulfilling her potential.

The successful primary school will be one in which children begin to understand something of the concern for others which is a characteristic of a civilized and truly caring society. It will be manifest in many ways. Are the teachers as open, honest and sympathetic to the anxieties of parents as they should be? Do the parents see the schools as a place of confrontation or one of comfort and mutual exploration? Do the teachers talk to children as though they really respected their uniqueness and integrity? Do parents and teachers actively and overtly show interest in those who do not embrace their faith, culture, creed and nationhood?

To come full circle, perhaps the most significant observation in the whole section of the Plowden Report on religious education concerns the part played in a child's spiritual development by the community of school, where he learns that 'charity is people'.

Part Three   *Contemporary Concerns*

10   The Role of the Local Authority

It is comforting, I always think, to realize that although schools are probably the commonest projection of government and state into people's lives, they are also accepted and their work, for the most part, is welcomed. A school in the centre of a small community gives a sense of purpose and direction to the lives of all who live around it. Perhaps it is because we live, subconsciously, through the lives and expectations of our young people that the observation that to close a village school is to kill the village contains more than just a grain of truth.*

Acknowledging the large degree of independence and autonomy enjoyed by our primary school should not, however, blind us to the fact that each school is part of a much larger organization and that there are many more services which are available to children, to parents and to teachers than can be obtained through one particular school. These services are provided by the local authority.

The local authority – which is responsible for many other services in addition to education † – is elected at a municipal election. From its councillors it appoints a committee to run education in its area, through the professionals it employs. The local authority will determine the amount of money available for the schools it is providing for and the ancillary services that are associated with them. Central government will, of course, lay down guidelines which local authorities must follow, but a great deal is left to local initiative. How mean – or how generous

*According to a survey conducted in 1977 by the Council for the Protection of Rural England over 500 primary schools were closed between 1967 and 1977 (a rate of one school per week). The Plowden Report recommended that a five to eleven year primary school should have a minimum of three classes containing sixty to eighty children.

† The only exception to this is the Inner London Education Authority, which has no other local government function.

– a local authority is will depend upon many factors. A rural community with many small schools to support in a sparsely populated area often finds it impossible on economic grounds to provide all the services that might be regarded as essential in a neat, middle-class dormitory suburb. In the latter, school swimming might be available to every child over seven; in the former – even in times of economic prosperity – such an idea is likely to remain for ever nothing more than an unrealistic dream.

I must stress that my observations on specialist services available to schools must be taken against this background – no two schools, no two education authorities, are identical and generalizations may well lead to misunderstanding.

Schools are staffed by teachers appointed by the local authority. They are also inspected by locally appointed advisers. These advisers (who in some areas are called inspectors) fulfil two roles. They have a pastoral function (in the sense that they try to help teachers with personal as well as professional problems) and they are also responsible for specific subject areas (like mathematics or English). It is also to the advisers that headteachers and teachers turn when they require help and advice in the development of particular areas of the curriculum, or when the teaching methods used in a school are under review. Each local authority adviser will be responsible for a certain number of schools within his area or for specific curriculum development in all schools run by the authority.

Usually the local advisory team work in close association with the wardens of teachers' centres and with advisory teachers. At the teachers' centres, teachers attend courses in individual curriculum areas and for professional and trades-union discussions. The role of both the teachers' centre warden and the advisers is to visit schools, to gain some understanding of local needs and to suggest ways of meeting them.

In addition to these professionals the local education authority will also employ a team of educational psychologists, psychiatric social workers, educational welfare officers and a medical officer of health, all of whom are responsible to the education officer. In turn the education officer is responsible to the elected members for all aspects of educational administration in the district, although in large towns and widespread county authorities this work is often delegated to divisional officers.

Alongside the local advisory team, but quite independent of them, work inspectors of schools appointed by the Department of Education and Science. These inspectors, known as HMIs, also fulfil a pastoral as well as a specialist function. The purpose of this duality is somewhat difficult to explain. It can be argued, however, that the HMI, because he is detached from local considerations, is able to give an informed 'over-view' of educational change and curriculum development and is less sensitive to local political pressures.

More immediate to the school's work are the non-professionals who spend their days working alongside the teachers – people, it should be said, who can exert just as profound an influence upon children as those who have been trained to do so.

A school is a community. The schoolkeeper and his cleaners, the secretary, the cook and the kitchen staff need to understand the aims and educational direction that the headteacher and staff are trying to follow as much as does the young probationary teacher straight from college. It is pointless trying to teach children the value of a quiet calm response when faced with a trying situation if, when the adults around them are similarly pressed, they explode in a neurotic frenzy.

Closest of all to the children are the infant and junior helpers. These are women workers whose job it is to assist the teacher in meeting children's needs – to help at the painting table or in the sewing corner, to mend books, to comfort children in distress, to supervise some play activities, to prepare material and look after stock. The task of training these helpers resides with the staff of the school. Very few courses for para-professionals in primary schools are available, even at local authority level.*

Between the professional workers in the education service

* The exception to this general rule is found in nursery classes, where assistants have to undergo a year's training.

and the parents there comes a third body – the managers or governors. Each school has a managing body of lay people who are meant to serve as a sounding board of local opinion, to watch over the school's curriculum and day-to-day running, to appoint staff, to be aware of the expenditure of public monies. The board is usually made up of members from the main political parties, the local authority, the parents and occasionally lecturers from colleges of education.

In September 1977 the Taylor Committee produced a report which has, at the time of writing, been much discussed but little implemented. Briefly the report recommended that each school should have a managing body made up, by equal representation, of parents, teachers, the local community and the education authority. To this body the local education authority would delegate responsibility for setting the broad aims of the school and in deciding how best to achieve them. The managers would also establish the procedures for dealing with difficult pupils, especially those who might find themselves excluded, suspended or expelled. The parent managers should be elected by parents at open meetings, and the teacher representatives should be elected by the staff. In order for such lay committees to be able to play a full part in the day-to-day running of a school, the committee further recommended that managers should attend locally based training courses.

The implications of these recommendations are far-reaching. Understandably the professional associations reacted with some reserve. The General Secretary of the National Union of Teachers doubted the wisdom of handing over the running of schools to 'management by unaccountable committee', but the Headmaster's Association welcomed the recommendations since they would 'help stop creeping bureaucracy and unwarranted political abuse of power in some local authorities'. The response from parent associations was enthusiastic. 'For the first time,' said Mr John Hale, secretary of the National Confederation of PTAs, 'parents will have an effective voice in the government of schools.'

Whatever view we take of the Taylor Report, it has been

suggested, quite firmly, that schools and schooling should not simply be left to the professionals, that the skill of the professional (teacher, educational psychologist or administrator) must be harnessed to meet local needs in a comprehensive and comprehensible way. Education can only be successful when all who know, work and live with children can be brought together to fulfil a common purpose – the development of each school so that it meets as fully as possible the intellectual, social and spiritual demands of each and every child who attends it.

To some extent the role played by the administrator (lay or professional) and the inspector is supportive – determining what action to take on major issues, facilitating change and interpreting these decisions in individual cases at local level. In this respect, educational administration protects schools and enables senior staff to concentrate upon teaching, rather than (for example) admission procedures, the state of the school garden or the transfer of children between schools in the district.

11 The Exceptional Child

In those countries where dogma obscures the innate differences between people, it might be politically expedient to observe that all children are born with the same potential, the same gifts, interests and aptitudes. In England such a viewpoint would have little support. We know from our own school days and from watching our own children and those of our neighbours grow and develop that no two children are the same. Yet for all our acceptance of difference and the attempts which schools make to meet individual needs, there are children who are so different from their fellows that they need specific and specialist educational provision. Of these, two groups deserve particular attention: the child who is handicapped, and the child who is so gifted that time spent on conventional school programmes causes boredom and frustration because of its lack of challenge. Let me deal with each in turn.

The local advisory team, to which I referred in Chapter 10, will usually contain some members who are experienced in the educational needs of the handicapped, for whom education in conventional schools would be impossible. The term 'handicapped' embraces children who are blind and partially sighted, physically handicapped, deaf and hard of hearing, mentally retarded or emotionally disturbed.

The adviser alone will not be in a position to decide upon the placement of children in special schools for the handicapped. He will take the advice of the Educational Psychologist, the school Medical Officer of Health, senior educational welfare workers – all of whom will contribute towards making a decision which is both realistic and humane. In some areas of the county local authorities provide both day and boarding schools for their handicapped children; in others there is a deliberate and conscious attempt to integrate all but the severely abnormal into ordinary day schools.

The report of the Warnock Committee (1978) recommended far greater integration of the handicapped child into the life of the community, as well as more deliberate efforts to integrate the handicapped into conventional schools. Practical difficulties will have to be overcome before this ideal is realized. Whether it is appropriate to admit a handicapped child into a 'normal' school will depend upon a number of factors. Is the school suitably equipped with toilets? Are appropriate ancillary services (for example nursing auxiliaries) available? Does the building have easy access? Can ramps be provided in addition to stairs? Are the doors and passageways wide enough for wheelchairs?

My experience in having children suffering from spina bifida learning alongside children who are physically 'normal' was amongst the most rewarding of my teaching career. Both groups of children benefitted. The 'handicapped' because they were able to work alongside their intellectual equals, the 'normal' children because they were given the opportunity to relate to children whose mobility, *as human beings*, was restricted. Both groups had identical roles to play. Both groups had to live and work in a school and to overcome all the emotional and intellectual problems that this entailed. Much the most significant part of this experiment was the effect it had upon the children who were not handicapped. For the first time many of them saw calipers and wheelchairs as equipment which helped people to be 'normal', rather than as symbols of abnormality.

Sadly not all handicapped children will be able to be integrated into conventional schools. The severely handicapped, those requiring careful nursing, the emotionally disturbed, the blind and the deaf need attention and facilities which the ordinary day school cannot (as yet) provide. The time is ripe, however, for determined attempts to be made to integrate the child who is intellectually handicapped (the educationally subnormal). These children are simply slow learners of limited intelligence. If the primary school aims at meeting children's needs it should be able, by flexible grouping, to meet the intellectual needs of slow learners, while allowing them to benefit from the varied social, cultural and sporting activities that are to be found in the well-run school.

The gifted child also presents a very real difficulty to the adults in his life, both to parents and teachers. If we are fortunate to be living alongside a child of intelligence who can read with fluency at five, explain square numbers at six and is blessed with a razor-sharp brain, how should we 'educate' him? To force such children to follow a conventional learning programme and function at the same level as other children of their own age is likely to bore them and perhaps cause them to rebel against school altogether. The alternative – to set such children apart to be taught as a selected elite – is a possible solution, although such insulation from the rough and tumble of the everyday life of school is hardly likely to help them integrate into their year group. In dealing with the child of above-average academic ability it is important to realize that growth is not uniform – that because a child is a fluent reader he is not necessarily socially confident, that because he can multiply mixed fractions at seven he is not necessarily emotionally mature.

The task of the school is to give the gifted child the opportunity to develop to the full in his areas of excellence and encourage him to work independently of his class mates whenever it is appropriate for him to do so. The individual pattern of work that will be followed will not exclude the child from the centres of interest or projects that the whole class as a group are following. Indeed in schools where individuals are expected to work at their own pace, the gifted and the less able are not made to see themselves as exceptional. The experienced teacher will expect from each child *no more* and *no less* than each child in her group is capable of giving. Praise and criticism will be based upon the realization of potential rather than the achievement of a 'norm' applied unrealistically to all the children in the class or in an age group.

Some schools are providing more than an individualized school programme for the gifted child. In the school in which I work, for example, we give children the opportunity to explore language in some depth. A group of nine, ten and eleven year olds meet before lunch each day to learn something of the craft of the writer, to study extracts from Chaucer, Shakespeare, Dickens and Eliot, to listen to verse, to explore choral speaking. There is, in my opinion, the need to give children of above-average ability the opportunity to challenge each other on an intellectual plane, to exchange ideas, to develop their appreciation of literature and mathematics.

Local education authorities, conscious no doubt of public unease at the lack of provision for the exceptionally gifted child in some of the schools they administer, are also beginning to make special provision by establishing holiday and weekend programmes. These courses, which cover a wide range of activities from music-making to mathematics and environmental studies, are usually staffed by the local inspectorate assisted by specially selected teachers. The children for such courses are drawn from a number of schools. They could, therefore, be criticized on the grounds that while special programmes undoubtedly develop the skills of the more able child, they do so in an exclusive way.

Just as schools make provision for the gifted child, many also try to meet the less able, the disturbed, the shy, the diffident. For some children, an individual programme (supervised by a specialist teacher) is all that will be required to help them overcome their problems. The most common area in which remedial children need tutorial support is reading. Some large primary schools, however, now have special classes (called sanctuary or nurture) where children who are emotionally disturbed are helped to build up an identity with a particular teacher. These children usually spend the majority of their time in school within the 'sanctuary unit'. Because the numbers in the 'sanctuary' are very small, relationships are easier to establish and maintain than in the traditional classroom.

Such units also enable the staff to observe closely the children in their care and to structure learning to meet individual needs (be these academic, emotional or social).

The educational content of the programme of sanctuary classes is very similar to that followed by the therapists who work in the education psychological service and in psychiatric clinics. Their value lies in the fact that children can be given the psychological support they need without them having to be taken to clinics outside the school for treatment. This in turn has the effect of reducing the tensions of parent and child and facilitates transfer back into the 'normal' school programme when treatment has been completed. Teachers in nurture groups and sanctuary units invariably work in close association with the school psychological, medical and social services.

Not all schools are large enough to provide specialist withdrawal classes of the kind described above, nor would all schools have a sufficient number of children to warrant such provision. Most local education authorities, therefore, provide classes for children with particular needs. These 'tutorial' classes, which are attended by children for two, three or four half days a week, give them more freedom than they could be allowed in the conventional classroom. The number of children attending any one session rarely exceeds six and, as in the nurture groups, great emphasis is placed upon the exploration of relationships both within the peer group and with the teacher (who is usually a trained play-therapist).

These two types of provision are sometimes supplemented by specialist visiting teachers who withdraw children for individual instruction. These peripatetic teachers concentrate upon particular curriculum areas – such as reading and language. They work in close co-operation with the school and the school's psychological service.

Support services of the type described here are on-going and are not bound by a child's attendance at a particular school. Robin, for example, was attending a tutorial class before he joined my present school. It was felt that such support as he was getting was valuable – but insufficient. With the agreement of the school psychologist he was also given the opportunity to work with the remedial reading teacher, who came into school for an hour and a half a week to give him additional help. The specialized programme she initiated was reviewed once a term by the class teacher, the educational psychologist and the tutorial teacher. Through continuous discussion and assessment Robin (and his parents) were helped towards a solution of his difficulties.

Such intensive (and expensive) professional aid might, at first sight, seem to be something of a luxury. I believe, however, that many an adolescent would be saved from the courts if sufficient attention could be given to the tensions that occur in the early years of schooling. In this connection it is pertinent to observe that inability to master the rudiments of reading and writing create a very real tension. To remain illiterate after seven years in an institution whose central purpose is the mastery of words can have an immeasurable effect upon the child's view of himself.

To some extent this brings us full circle. Schooling is a way of preparing the younger members of society for the working world they will eventually enter. To educate *en masse* is obviously more efficient in terms of manpower and resources than to attempt to educate each child on an individual, personalized basis. The success of any system, however, can be measured by the degree of its response to individual needs and circumstance.

It is here that the parents of a child attending a primary school in England can count themselves more fortunate than the majority of their contemporaries across the world. For the English primary school system is possessed of an inbuilt flexibility which allows for individual initiative and local response to local needs.

For primary schools in England the decade between 1965 and 1975 was one of innovation, experiment and change. On its publication in 1967 the Plowden Report was well received and its proposals welcomed. Here (it seemed to those of us who were working in schools at the time) was a wise and thoughtful document. It confirmed something which we knew from experience and felt in our bones – that the freer approaches to the teaching of young children which were being practised in our schools provided the sort of starting point all children needed and deserved.

In approving changes that had taken years of slow development to achieve and by focusing attention upon them, the publication of the report also produced an unfortunate side effect. In some schools it resulted in the indiscriminate introduction of a plethora of new approaches to curriculum, timetabling and organization.

I do not wish to suggest that the Plowden Report was wrong or its members naïve idealists. Time and time again Lady Plowden and the members of her committee have spelt out in no uncertain terms that the document was, in many ways, a visionary one. Statements such as 'Schools are not teaching shops ... they must transmit values and attitudes' were always balanced by others (far less widely quoted) which stressed the need for schools also to be guardians of the more traditional values, 'neatness, accuracy, care, perseverance and the sheer knowledge which is an essential of being educated'.

From time immemorial the visionary and the prophet have been misunderstood (or only half heard) and in recent years the principles underlying the Plowden Report have come under increasing criticism. Education, we have been told, is not about attitudes and feelings, it is not about the romance of childhood.

It is about teaching children the skills they will eventually need in the world of work.

The Plowden Report might have been welcomed by professionals working in schools and educational administrations, but if the community was never helped to understand, if many teachers used it to excuse their own ineffective and outrageous practice, if parents were never given the opportunity to see its recommendations implemented in their local school or refused to see the vital link the report stressed between the expectations of home and the expectations of school – is it surprising that there has been a backlash, a demand for a return to the more traditional approaches to the teaching of young children?

At its very core the philosophy that Plowden represents is the belief that schools should be caring communities where each child is given the opportunity to develop his gifts to the full, to grow through childhood into adolescence and adulthood beyond. It saw the school as part of a society which will 'care for all its members, for the old as well as the young, for the handicapped as well as the gifted, for the deviant as well as the conformer', in a climate that was 'stimulating, honest and tolerant'. This society would (hopefully!) not be 'too engrossed with the pursuit of material wealth, too hostile to minorities, too dominated by mass opinion and too uncertain of its values'. Ten years on and the brave new world heralded by Plowden looks as much a pipe dream as it did when the report was first published, for schools cannot operate in isolation from the society which they serve. It is impossible to project reading in school as an enriching hobby if, at home, books are regarded as things that television serials are based upon; it is impossible to make Jean understand that stealing is wrong if her mother makes ends meet by shoplifting, or to persuade Peter that football is a game if his big brother is one of a gang that takes an array of weapons to the local football match every Saturday throughout the season.

Yet, despite these reservations, despite the disenchantment, the Plowden Report opened the way for change, for it provided the most comprehensive survey of primary education in England that had ever been undertaken. It enabled all who were interested in the education of young children – parents, students, teachers, academics – to obtain an overall picture of life in a primary school, its curriculum and the place of the young child in the society of school, home and community. If this has helped improve society's understanding of the purpose of primary education it has also served to make society more critical of its obvious shortcomings, more intolerant of its mistakes.

The next ten years will probably see a subtle change in the control of our schools, a change that will have the effect of strengthening the good practice which Plowden observed while preventing the excesses to which child-centred education, thoughtlessly applied, can lead.

Although I do not foresee the imposition of a narrow-core curriculum of the type followed by most developed countries of the world, moves are already being made which suggest that teachers will be expected to become more accountable for the curriculum that is followed in their schools.

To some extent, of course, teachers are already accountable to their local education authority. This has always been so. Headteachers, though enjoying considerable freedom in the way in which they organize their schools, are still ultimately responsible for its wellbeing and efficiency. Like all teachers they are bound by the contracts that are exchanged on appointment.

Nor should we dismiss as insignificant the power which the local authority can wield should it come into conflict with the staff of a school. Evidence of this is provided by the ILEAs internal inquiry into the William Tyndale School in 1976. Here, teaching staff, parents, managing body and the authority itself were in conflict, a conflict which revolved around one central issue – who should be responsible *in the last resort* for how a child spends his day in school. Is it the authority, through the advisory team of inspectors? Is it the headteacher and his staff? Is it the parents as represented on the managing body? However one views the report of the inquiry, one thing is crystal clear, real power lay, not with teachers, but with the elected members of the authority who saw it as their responsibility to ensure that schools functioned in a manner and to a standard acceptable to the parents whose children spent their days there. The head and the majority of the teaching staff were publicly censured and dismissed.

Fortunately Tyndale was an extreme case. No intelligent person would suggest that inquiries chaired by eminent lawyers are a satisfactory way of keeping a teaching force in check. For one thing the majority of teachers are far from extravagant in their methods and far more traditional than critics of primary schools would have the general public believe. This is borne out by the most recent survey of primary schools * by Her Majesty's Inspectorate which suggests that 75 per cent of teachers use traditional didactic methods in their classrooms, 5 per cent discovery methods, while the remainder employ a mixture of these two approaches.

Such figures, however, can lull society at large into complacency, particularly when they are linked (as happened in this survey) with statistics to show that standards in basic subjects were rising.

A school should not be singled out for criticism simply because it is using discovery methods. The formal school can be just as intellectually crippling a place to live in for a young child as one in which the methods are extravagantly free. In my opinion the most satisfactory way of achieving control of its schools by the community is to make headteachers far more accountable for their stewardship to their local authority than is at present the case.

This could be achieved by giving headteachers contracts for a fixed number of years instead of for life. This contract (of seven or ten years) would be renewable. If terminated, the head could return to the classroom or apply for a headship elsewhere. At present the professional bodies (particularly the National Association of Headteachers) refuse to consider such a suggestion on the grounds that to take away contract for life would

Primary Education in England: A Survey by HM Inspectors of Schools, HMSO, 1978.

diminish the effectiveness of their members (of whom, I should add, I am one). This is to ignore one significant weakness of life tenure. The enthusiastic headteacher of forty can so easily become the somnolent, desk-bound executive of fifty-five. Appointment for life in a job so important for the well-being of a school and its children is a luxury I do not think our society is able to afford.

Some countries already appoint principal or headteachers for defined terms of years. In Yugoslavia, for example, the head of an elementary school can expect to work for two three-year terms in one institution. Headteachers who find administration frustrating and irksome can easily slip back into the classroom without loss of face, and given a reasonable interchange of staff at head/senior teacher level those principals who are not offered re-appointment do not seem to find their change of status too hard to bear.

There is one further point worth considering. A teacher is appointed to the position of head because he or she has outstanding ability as a teacher. When teachers become heads, the nature of their administrative role results in their being able to spend much less time on the work (teaching) which singled them out for promotion.

If headteachers were accountable to the local authority, they would also be more accountable to their managing body. Managing bodies, and the part they can play in the development of a school, came under close scrutiny by the Taylor Committee. The committee's report emphasized the part which parents should play on the governing (management) boards of schools. If parents could be encouraged to become effective and informed managers of our schools (in place of the nominees of political parties), then matters of common concern could be discussed between head, teacher and parent representatives in a more frank and open way than occurs at the moment. Without seeming to be critical of the governing body of the school in which I work, I do sometimes find myself asking the following questions. Should a state school have on the committee people whose sole reason for attendance is membership of a political party, whose own children have never attended a state school, who have never been on a training course in school management, who never attend school functions and who don't even live in the district? I suggest it is because management bodies are ill-equipped to discuss the problems and expectations of the professionals working in the schools that there is considerable resentment on the part of teachers at suggestions (like the one I have made on headship appointments) for an increase in their powers.

If the managing body is the outward and visible sign of community representation in school, parents also influence the way a school works and exercise a subtle control upon the teachers. This influence might be hidden – but it is persuasive nevertheless. Why, in areas where there is a choice of schools, do parents choose one school rather than another? Mainly, I would suggest, because that school reflects the values (for music, painting, informality, old-fashioned discipline or whatever) that the parents themselves hold dear. Where there is no choice the parents effect change on a school by gentle pressure, by establishing a 'friends of the school' association, by political pressure through the management body. The sad thing is that often the schools which are in most need of change, most in need of community support, are in those parts of the country where the community is unlikely to contribute.

Accountability also implies the maintenance of standards and this task obviously cannot be undertaken by a lay committee of school governors. Can the day to day work of a school be monitored and if so how can this best be done?

This task may not be as daunting, time consuming or destructive as it may first appear. Both the Department of Education and local education authorities have ways of assessing the performance of schools. Most local authorities, for example, set standardized tests to facilitate transfer at eleven. The scores so obtained indicate performance in reading, writing and number, and these, when related to the community that the school is serving, go some way to measuring a school's success in 'basic skill' areas. Knowledge of the local community is of paramount importance when examining these figures, for scores on an IQ paper or arithmetic test cannot be used as the only criteria when comparing one school with another.

For one school in a predominately middle-class area to get higher marks for mathematics and English than a neighbouring school which serves an identical population is not to make the first school better than the second. If children attending the first school are brought up on nothing more than a diet of sums and comprehension tests while those attending the second have a much more liberal programme it might well be argued that the second school is a far better place for young people to develop their skills and talents. Neither do test scores alone tell anything about the stability and experience of teaching staff of different schools or the varying facilities available on different school sites.

Assessment at local level can take into account all the variables and an experienced advisory team should be able to measure adequately the performance of all the schools in their area.

Nationally there is also a need to keep a check upon attainment and curriculum development. The Department of Education and Science also employs a team of inspectors who are in a position to assess the needs and achievements of particular areas and set them within a broader national framework. Such assessment need not mean tests at seven and eleven (as has been suggested by at least one prominent Conservative); indeed such testing would, in my opinion, be destructive of much that English primary education has achieved since 1945. The green paper *Education in Schools, a Consultative Document*, published by the Department of Education and Science in July 1977, observes that 'inspection is a subjective and qualitative process, although HM Inspectorate is increasingly moving towards complementary quantitative analyses' of which the Assessment of Performance Unit (APU) is one example.

This unit has concentrated upon the development of tests suitable for national monitoring in English language, mathematics and science. A programme of national assessment began in May 1978 and concerned itself with the standards of mathematics achieved by eleven year olds. This programme was extended to include fifteen year olds in November 1978 and will be further extended to language (in 1979) and science (in 1980). The Assessment of Performance Unit's task is to provide a national picture of pupil performance and an indication of how performance is changing over time. It will not produce information on the attainment of individual pupils or schools. In monitoring performance nationally it will not be necessary to test every pupil. Only a very small proportion of pupils in selected age groups in primary and secondary schools will be tested or assessed over a small part of the curriculum. This will give a representative national picture. The method of testing is explained by the Department of Education and Science in a series of leaflets. In *Facts and Figures about Monitoring*, we learn that 'Selection for testing will be by reference to a pupil's date of birth. Performance in mathematics and language will be assessed at 11 (that is, pupils whose 11th birthday falls during the year in which testing takes place) and 15, early in the final year of compulsory schooling. Science will be assessed at 11, 13 and 15 and the first modern foreign language probably at 13 only. Out of each age group (about 700,000 children) about 12,000 (1.7 per cent) will be tested each year for each aspect of the curriculum.

'To ensure that the APU monitoring exercise covers a representative sample of pupils across the country, about 1,000 primary and about 500 secondary schools may be asked to take part in each exercise in any one year. In other words, 5 per cent of schools with 11 year olds and 10 per cent of schools with 15 year olds will be included. About one third of the 11 year olds or one sixth of the 15 year olds will be tested each year in any one school in the sample for each aspect of the curriculum.'

It is proposed to publish separate reports for each aspect of the curriculum monitored and for each age group tested. Each report will describe in detail the basis of the assessment. The results will be analysed, and tabulated where relevant and appropriate, by sex of pupil; school size and type; location (metropolitan or non-metropolitan area); and region. It may also be possible to analyse the results against indices of social disadvantage. The sample size will be stated and the extent to which the various findings are statistically reliable will be reported.

Accountability, however, will not simply be imposed upon schools from above. The Taylor Report suggested that the managing body should also oversee the curricula. In the light of this recommendation the staffs of schools are likely to be more concerned than ever before in monitoring their own performance against the goals that they themselves set. In 1977 the Inner London Education Authority published a set of guidelines for teachers, entitled *Keeping the School under Review*. In the foreword Guy Rogers, the Deputy Chief Inspector, observes that 'the danger in any form of self-assessment is that people do not always see themselves as others see them'. With the object of defining the strengths and weaknesses of their own school the leaflet suggests a range of questions that might be asked – some of which parents might also ask about the school that their own child attends. These include:

1. What provision is there for gifted children, slow learners, those with behavioural problems, those with a specific skill or talent, those from different ethnic backgrounds?

2. What opportunities are given for the development of initiative and responsibility?

3. Who is responsible for promoting continuity in the various areas of the curriculum?

4. What attention is given to the use of individual apparatus and materials and differences in learning and teaching styles?

5. Are there obstacles to achieving continuity in learning?

6. What initiatives are taken to introduce the school to parents?

7. How is the school developing links with the neighbourhood?

8. Is there an effective Parent Teacher Association?

9. How does the school co-operate with other educational

agencies (e.g. Adult Evening Institute, Polytechnics, Colleges of Further Education)?

10. How is the school organized?

11. How is progress in literacy and mathematics assessed?

12. Who is responsible for ensuring that the school is kept in a state of workmanlike tidiness?

13. Who ensures that displays of work are well mounted and regularly changed?

14. Are we clear as to what we are trying to do?

15. Would I recommend a colleague to apply for a post in the school and would I recommend the school to friends for their children?

Accountability at local level will bring in its wake a new dialogue. To meet the new demands that will be made upon them the schools will have to become places which include (rather than exclude) the whole community. Where this has happened already, the traditional role of the teacher is beginning to change. If the school is a community centre need all the staff be teachers? Would a community worker function better than a teacher as an initiator of out of school activities? If part of the school site is to be used for youth work with eight to seventeen year olds during evenings, weekends and holidays, would the youth worker be more effective if he were a member of the school staff rather than employed through a Youth Office at the local town hall?

Just as we should look at the function of professionals working in the community, we will need to look at the periods of time that they spend there. Is there an acceptable reason for our current three-term year, nine-to-four day? Does this traditional pattern make for effective and efficient teaching and learning? Does it make best use of expensive community investment? Some schools are already experimenting by appointing teachers to work an 'extended' day;* others co-operate on holiday

---

* A teacher working an extended day might work from 10.30 am to 7.30 pm on four days a week, or work only in the afternoons and evenings. The pattern is determined by local needs.

schemes which use school facilities during periods when they would otherwise lie dormant.

The move of school into community should not be seen as an isolated gesture. It will be reciprocated by a move of the community into the school. The degree to which parents can become involved in a school varies so much from community to community that it is impossible to discuss here the effects that this might have upon the teaching force. But already anxiety has been expressed by the professional associations about the system of open documentation that is being introduced by some local authorities. If we cannot write in confidence about children without fear of their parents disagreeing with our observations, argue the teachers, then we are less likely to give forceful and direct written opinions for colleagues to follow up on transfer to another class, another school or another authority. To which I would respond that if education is a partnership between parent and teacher then we, the teachers, must learn how to communicate with parents in a more direct way than we have hitherto managed to do. Our records in school will need to be supported by cumulative evidence of a child's progress over the years of his stay in primary school, and this – rather than hurriedly written child studies – will increasingly form the basis of parent-teacher discussions. If written reports which remain with the child's records are to be open to parents then such information which is exchanged between schools is much more likely to be accurate and the quality of its presentation and content more considered than has sometimes been the case. It is far too easy for the class teacher to become subjective in her writing, to use emotive phrases to conjure up in the reader her personal picture of a child. The advent of open reports should encourage teachers to be more coolly rational in their observations on children – and for this reason alone are to be welcomed.

Community involvement is also likely to bring with it some new responsibility – particularly towards children of pre-school age. At present the primary school is legally bound to accept children at the beginning of the term that falls after their fifth birthday, although in practice many 'rising fives' * are admitted. But over the country as a whole provision for children of pre-school age is quite haphazard and irregular. Nursery schools and classes abound in some areas, in others the allocation of public funds to pre-school education is derisory. Unless the current population trend is reversed, the next ten years will see a radical fall in the size of the school population. This will mean that some schools will either become too small to remain viable institutions in an economic sense, or that the school places which become available will be given to younger children – that each primary school will run, for example, a class for four to five year olds, attendance at which is voluntary (a Kindergarten stage). Such a move would quieten the anxiety of educationalists who, while wishing to foster pre-school education, fear that the spread of the play group movement (which, being a voluntary association, makes little demand upon public funds) has encouraged successive governments to do nothing to extend state provision and meet the objections of political economists who see no reason to expand children's services at a time when the labour market is slack.†

There will obviously be changes on the way the curriculum develops. After ten years of innovation and change it is likely that there will be a period of consolidation. Buildings will continue to be adapted to meet the changing demands of the curriculum. Open-plan schools – the answer to the changes brought about by a free, experimental curricula – are still being built, but the openness is more circumscribed, there are more small rooms for individual study and project work and the open classrooms are more intimate, less barn-like.

If these developments reflect the changes that have already emerged into the curriculum (as I believe they do) then they

* Children who will reach their fifth birthday during the term.

† Nursery provision is most likely to be expanded when the state has need to employ female labour for economic or political reasons. In Yugoslavia, for example, mothers can place their children in nursery units from the age of six months, depositing them as early as 5.30 am and collecting them between 4.30 and 5.30 pm.

will continue and accelerate. Educational hardware – tape recorders, television sets, video machines, individual learning programmes through aural and visual aids – has not really found a firm foothold in our schools. But many primary schools now have libraries where once they had book trollies, a music room where once they had only a piano and many a language laboratory has grown from a single tape recorder. Invariably specialization of equipment is likely to result in a curtailing of some freedoms. A dark room houses expensive equipment and cannot be left open to the world; a pottery kiln has many safety devices built into it, but it needs to be handled with responsibility and considerable care. Perhaps we should beware lest machines become ever more dominant in our schools, for the machine, however sophisticated, will never be able to replace the personal contact with an adult which enables a child to develop an understanding of himself and his world.

The advent of technology might also have the effect of reopening the debate on language teaching in schools. French is taught by the direct method in some primary schools, but if the observations of secondary school teachers are anything to go by, it were best if French had never been introduced into the primary school curriculum at all. Against this must be set the evidence from schools in other countries where 'immersion programmes' in a foreign language can take up as much as one entire primary school year. My personal view is that the primary school child is already being asked to participate in a sufficient range of activities and that to make even further demands would be bordering on the irresponsible.

A more likely change in curriculum content – and one which would be both responsible and acceptable – lies in the field of multi-cultural and religious studies. Schools in England are now beginning to educate the children of second-generation immigrants, children who, although they owe some allegiance to the country of their birth, also have a cultural and spiritual allegiance to a non-Western, non-Christian way of life. The European Economic Community has recognized the problems faced by the children of migrant workers, and member countries are able to obtain EEC funding to provide facilities in schools to teach 'mother tongues' and provide the opportunity for such children to learn about the history, culture and religious practices * of their people.

It is obvious, I think, that we cannot sit back and talk grandly about multi-cultural education and do nothing. Neither should we expect parents whose roots lie in the West Indies, Africa and the Indian subcontinent to continue to accept that Western Christian values or Western Christian history have great significance or much relevance to their children. This might mean that more resources will have to be made available to specific areas of the country. Positive discrimination was recommended by the Plowden Committee to help alleviate social and environmental handicap. It may be that the next decade will see positive support being given to non-Christian communities so that cultures can be preserved and the rifts and tensions which have developed between our different religious and ethnic communities healed.

Some change of emphasis is foreshadowed in government White Paper 7186 which recommends that future educational statistics should be collected on an ethnic basis, a significant departure from the usual practice. This must be seen against the findings of recent research † which seems to suggest that West Indian children are lagging further behind their white classmates in literacy at the end of their school career than they were at the beginning. Alan Little, Lewisham Professor of Social Administration at Goldsmith's College, examined how 11,000 white and 1,400 West Indian children fared in three consecutive Inner London Education Authority surveys. He compared the performance of the same group of children as they grew from eight to fifteen.

* In Sweden, a non-EEC member, all immigrant children are taught the language of their homeland, its history and customs in the same way as other school subjects.

† *Education Policies for Multi-Racial Areas*, Alan Little, Goldsmith's College, London.

London: reading test scores at 8, 11 and 15 (National mean = 100)

	All children of West Indian origin	West Indians fully educated UK	White children from unskilled homes	All children of UK origin
1968 (aged 8)	87·8	89·9	93·7	98·4
1971 (aged 11)	87·4	88·7	93·5	98·6
1975 (aged 15)	85·9	87·1	92·1	98·2

Little does not attribute these figures to genetic differences in white and black children, because West Indians educated wholly in this country do better than more recent immigrants. The most important influence, he suggests, are the teachers. Teachers tend to stereotype West Indians by expecting poor work and bad behaviour, causing the children to live down to their teachers' expectations. He does not blame the teachers for this, for they are only reflecting the attitudes of the dominant British culture which tends to deny the West Indians a sense of their own ethnic and cultural identity. This conflict is also pinpointed in the government White Paper, which notes that 'Pupils from various minority groups face specific difficulties arising from linguistic, cultural, religious and historical differences. We must compensate for these difficulties if such pupils are to be given the same range of opportunity and choice as indigenous pupils. The aim must be that a growing number of those from the ethnic minorities should seek and achieve positions of influence.'

One other likely development is the establishment of links between primary schools and the secondary schools which they feed. At the moment such links are fairly minimal and usually consist of occasional visit by primary children and teachers to the neighbouring secondary schools. In some areas primary school teachers are moving into the secondary school to work for a year to help ease the emotional pressures which some-times occur on transfer. In other areas the links involve the interchange of staff for part of each week through the first term or the first year – a secondary teacher teaching for half a week in the primary school, while the primary teacher works with her 'old class' in the secondary school.

In recent years such arrangements have become increasingly essential, for as primary method has become less and less tradi-tional, the gulf between the two stages has become increasingly wide, and an understanding by both groups of teachers of the aims and aspirations of their colleagues working at different levels in the education service has come to be of paramount importance.

Finally, the English primary school must meet its most significant and immediate challenge. It must demonstrate quietly and effectively that education is about children, for herein lies its strength to meet and harness change. If it fails, then a system will be imposed upon it and our children (and our nation) will be that much the poorer.

Index